SIGNED

Beyond Reflecting

Actions Lead to Personal Potential

Gary Ray Gasaway

To go beyond reflecting you must act. Take actions today that will lead you to your personal potential tomorrow...

Gary

DEDICATION

To all those that realize without action, there is no growth, nor opportunity to strive for personal potential. A perfect example would include the famous author; William Shakespeare, who wrote *King Lear* while being quarantined because of the black plague in 1563. With nothing to do but act or remain idle, Shakespeare chose to take compelling and committed actions. As for me, I wrote the draft to this book during my own quarantine time concerning the Covid-19 Pandemic in the early months of 2020. The point I am making is that without actions there are no results. Even going beyond reflecting regarding our life's experiences are really just good intentions. It is only when we take compelling and committed actions according to those experiences that we strive toward growth and our personal potential.

To my mother, Lenore 'Mickie' Taylor, who pushed me early on in life to take committed actions in school, at work, and overall life. One of her favorite motivators was to apprise me on the fact that success in life was built upon actions. Once you accomplish something, look for the next opportunity. I often think about her toughness, her outlook upon life, and her tenacity that lives within me. I would like to think about her life as it came to an end from a lyric regarding a great song

...

– *"she went down swingin"* –
Tom Petty

CONTENTS

ACKNOWLEDGMENTS

To my love, my partner, and maybe my toughest critic; Kimberly, my wife. It is through our dedicated actions that have provided us both learning and growth opportunities which developed in harmony within our relationship. It has been a wonderful experience that I reflect upon daily and one that continues to blossom.

To my children – Shandee, Brit, Emily, and Cady – may this book, as in the previous books, be a constant reminder that it is through your actions that make both learning and growth possible. And for that reason, never stop taking committed actions to grow for it is a lifelong journey to strive for your personal potential.

To my siblings – Susie and Steve – who's loving support is 'family strong' - thank you as always for being a special part of my continued journeys. To my brother, James, your strong spirit continues to light up the stars above.

To Kimberly La Porte, Emily Ann, Cady Pranke, and Shandee Rae as you all did such wonderful work in editing and proofreading my material. Your own growth regarding this craft has been exciting to witness!

Finally, to all my friends as they continue to show love, support, and inspire me to do my absolute best.

Gary Ray Gasaway

INTRODUCTION

Are you ready to take the next step to truly getting something out of what you reflect upon daily? You may ask yourself, why reflection? Well, we do more than just think about our lives, we reflect upon them in a purposeful way. In fact, consciously or unconsciously, we are always reflecting.

If you responded with a *yes* to the question of getting something out of what you reflect upon (or even if you are not sure), you are about to embark on a journey that will greatly change what you do with these reflections. In this book, I will guide you through a straightforward, but simple way to improve your life. How? By simply going beyond mere reflecting to taking necessary actions regarding your reflective experiences. What will be the results of these actions? Glad you asked. Two things. One is growth, and second, a continuous forward movement toward your personal potential. Well, sounds exciting!

But what is personal potential? We have all heard the phrase – full potential. Well, I have the opinion that there is no such thing as *full potential*. I don't think we ever truly reach the pinnacle of our maximum potential, but I do believe we can attain our own *personal potential*. So, I refer to our potential as *personal*. Why is this? It is because we are all unique. We all have a different potential, personal to us, only to us as individuals. So, it's taking a journey of self-discovery regarding our reflective experiences, engaging into committed actions, thus learning from these actions, and then leading us to growth. And, oh by the way, striving toward our personal potential at the same time.

In fact, everything you are about to read is based upon ordinary and practical methods, techniques, and principles for successful results. And what exactly are these ordinary and practical methods, techniques, and principles? They are from a history of tried and true-life experiences and observations. But do they actually work? Well, only if you're willing to do something to change your life. Wait, willing to do something? What am I talking about? It is the one thing that hinders our learning, stops our growth, and the potential for a better life. That *one thing* is acting on what we reflect upon. Will these *actionable* methods, techniques, and principles truly work? The short answer is – yes. In fact, they will change your life.

Now that I have your attention, would you like to know how? The 'how' is easy, it derives from just average people, like you and me. Yes indeed, anyone can learn to take appropriate actions to strive for their own individual personal potential. It's by taking appropriate actions, that growth is realized, and this then creates the path to personal potential. The point I am making is that anyone can create the actions they choose from the reflective experiences in their life. It's only possible by taking the right steps that go beyond our reflections which then leads to growth and forward efforts toward our personal potential. So, other than my own personal experience, is that the *actionable* methods, techniques, and principles that I will share in this book will result in success ONLY if you use them. As in all the books that I have written, the subjects I articulate, there is nothing that will be more personally satisfying as implementing the information and realizing your own individual results. Believe me, it works!

As a former corporate trainer, and now a professional life coach and speaker, I know many of the topics we reflect upon, along with the experiences that we should, but many times don't take the appropriate actions to improve our lives. I have in the past, and still do today, facilitate and train my audiences on subjects that are focused upon improving things like: employee performance, conflict resolution, managing stress, relationship building, time management, self-improvement, and to help develop and sustain motivation. All in creating more joyful and fulfilled lives. Sounds good, right? And for the most part, these speaking engagements are truly effective. Moreover, I would wager that once leaving these facilitations, most of the participants were elated and motivated to implement these new *people skills* they had learned. In fact, through personal feedback, many individuals in my audiences shared that they had made at least temporary, positive changes in their lives, while others took this newfound information and made some immediate changes that stayed with them for a bit longer.

But the problem with any training, coaching, or facilitating is that within a few weeks, even a month or two, most of these individuals went right back to the way they were before attending one of these sessions. (By the way, I have always believed to keep motivation alive, we must act upon it. That is an important part of this book. It's about taking compelling and committed actions. We will get into that later.)

So, why is it that these individuals don't take this promising information and continually act upon it? Is it because they didn't care? Did they get too busy? I don't believe it's a case of not caring or too busy. I believe that most people just want to move on to *the next new thing* before truly implementing something long-term into their lives.

In this book, I take the approach of expressing the information that is written to be embraced and sustaining. Yes! It's about producing long-lasting, sustainable positive results that will, again if you put into practice, will help you grow, and in turn move you forward toward your personal potential. It's truly about reading and embracing the material

3

in this book, taking the information I share with you, implementing this information, then growing from the experience.

The journey begins with our reflective experiences that leads us to our thoughts, purpose, learning, self-improvement, and finally to our personal growth. All of this in striving toward our personal potential. Even if you did not read my previous book regarding reflecting: *The Reflection Connection – Reflecting and Connecting to Life's Experiences*, this journey will be well worth your time and effort. But, of course, I recommend reading that book as well. In this book, I will briefly introduce main topics from the first manuscript regarding reflections so that you will have a solid foundation concerning the importance of reflecting and connecting. Furthermore, how to move beyond merely responding to your reflections, to taking committed actions, thus growth, which helps us strive toward our personal potential.

The only way to make this information into a true learning experience is to embrace it and take all the necessary actions that are well-laid out for you throughout the book. What will be the results? You will go beyond reflective responses, moving you into actions, thus realizing individual growth. All of which moves you closer to your own individual personal potential.

CHAPTER 1

WHAT IS REFLECTION CONNECTION?

If we are going to discuss how actions lead us to personal potential, we must begin where it all starts, and that is through reflecting upon our life's experiences. This process, of what I refer to as 'reflection connection', provides the foundation to understanding why reflecting is a vital stage before taking actions. It will be the level of effectiveness of going beyond merely reflecting upon our experiences to taking the necessary actions associated with the reflective experiences that will produce both learning and growth.

Briefly, reflection connection is a process of deeply thinking, feeling, and responding to all our experiences in life. As it is truly a cycle, it must have a beginning to start, work or efforts, and ending with a result.

This cycle can be summed up by our thoughts regarding an event or situation, moving to feelings, then developing a variety of different responses to the experience. This cycle is only the foundation for learning and growth to occur. As I stated, there is a beginning (thoughts and feelings) and an end (response, or result). What's missing is the work, or efforts in the middle that create a gap between thinking and the results of those thoughts. This work is the actions you take from your reflective experiences to produce growth (the new, enhanced result.)

It's the gap between the thoughts and the results are where the actions take place. These gaps, if you would, are also filled with various barriers and obstacles that are part of the natural progression to get to these actions. In fact, these barriers and obstacles are all throughout the process of the reflective experience; hence the work that must be done to have an effective result.

This book, and its contents, is designed to go beyond this simple process of just reflecting to making decisions, but to act upon our experiences with compelling and committed actions to learn and grow from them. As we will continue to grow from these experiences, thus the wonderful opportunity for striving toward our personal potential is now possible.

What about this connection? Well, connecting to our reflections creates a solid attachment to whatever reflective experience that we are thinking about. It's an attachment because of its importance. Now, regarding most of these important experiences, there is some associated, compelling action required.

That's where this book comes in. Helping us to understand the important steps to follow by asking the questions of: What stops us from taking action? What are the barriers and obstacles involved? What about learning from these reflective experiences? Self-improvements? Are there specific steps to taking action to grow? You want the answers? Keep reading! These questions and more will be answered throughout this book!

Let's go back to the idea of connections for a moment. There are some connections stronger than others, but all of what we think about becomes some level of connection. I refer to this process as *thinking about what you're thinking about*. It's a purposeful progression that; unfortunately, many of us don't take the necessary time, nor effort to do effectively. But why reflecting? It is because we begin with reflecting upon life's experiences in order to respond or take appropriate actions upon them; thus, for learning and growing to take shape. It's that old saying – *think before you act*. But, if this process is done ineffectively, without the necessary insightful and purposeful thoughts or feelings, the actions we take will also suffer. So, let's go into more detail regarding these reflective experiences.

We Begin with Asking Questions

Do you reflect upon your life? The answer is yes. We all do. But do we experience purposeful reflection connections that create better self-awareness and develop plans to take committed actions to promote enrichment in our lives? The answer unfortunately is few truly experience the essential and wonderful stage of effective reflection – connecting with them.

For most, our reflecting derives from unconscious efforts of unintentional thoughts. Why not create purposeful reflections – ones that you truly connect to? It is purposeful reflection connections that allow us to shape our thoughts, inspire and stretch our feelings, and create responses that promote self-awareness. And if this self-awareness is embraced and applied to the real possibility of learning, it leads us to take committed actions that move us to our personal growth. This then produces enrichment in our lives as we strive for our personal potential.

Again, it is the cycle of connecting with our reflections that begins with our thoughts and feelings regarding an experience we wish to reflect upon. With thoughts and feelings created, the reflection then moves to an effective response. It is with effectiveness of the response that provides the level of connection you will experience from your reflection.

In this book, we will go beyond this cycle of thinking, feeling, and simply responding to our reflections. If put into perspective, it is not just one thought, feeling, and response after the other, but one becomes the other. In other words, it's a melting pot of various phases of possibilities to actions that are created through our reflections.

Of course, most of us don't go about it in this fashion; hence this book. We will go where many of us barely touch the surface but go beyond reflecting to take effective actions regarding our experiences that move us to learning and then growth. The results? A continuous effort to strive for our personal potential.

In short, reflection connection is created intentionally to embrace your thoughts and express your feelings. These thoughts and feelings lead to responding with authority for this creates the foundation of connecting to life experiences. Reflection connection is the most effective way to engage self-awareness that results in enriching your life. In other words, instead of letting the world create you, you direct the paths of your own world through reflection. With reflection connection, you can discover the real peace and fulfillment you seek in your life.

Our Inner Drive

In this book, we go beyond the simple cycle of thoughts, feelings, and responses. Here, we take a deep dive into creating reflection connections that promote compelling and committed actions that will lead to personal potential. These types of connections will need energy or drive behind them to be most effective. So, these reflection connections are all about your inner drive of *being*, which in turn, affects your outer drive of *doing*. Okay, let's pause there for a moment. You say inner and outer drives?

Let's define them first. Inner drive. You say, drive? Yes, it is this drive that strongly indicates activeness and assertiveness. This drive, as I refer to, is more than an intent to do something, it's a confirmation to do it. Further, it's not what you do, but it is how you do what you do determines whether you are fulfilling your destiny. And how you do what you do is determined by your inner drive. Yes. The 'how' is designed by and a confirmation of our thoughts and feelings, or our inner drive. In other words, the 'how' is the confirmation, energy, and motivation to move to actions. So, once our inner drive is examined and prepared, we then move to the next step, our outer drive. We can now take the necessary actions to promote learning, then personal growth that will guide us to our personal potential.

Our Outer Drive

What about this outer drive? Our outer drive goes beyond our thoughts and feelings from our inner drive within. As explained referencing to our inner drive, now enters our outer drive. Once our inner drive provides us the confirmation, energy, and motivation to implement an outward movement of actions, we are now ready for *doing*. It is this *doing* that is associated with the actions you take that begins with your inner drive of *being*. This deep, intentional process allows you to make better sense of your present existence and the opportunity to create the world that could be. This creating is the *doing*, or actions you complete to learn, grow, and then strive for your personal potential.

Reflective Memories

When we think of reflecting upon our lives, many of us will focus on those memories that made unique impacts upon our lives. Unfortunately, not all memories are positive events. Our reflections are a continuous series of good and bad. It is a reality that there are both successes and failures in life. Yes, there are many occasions while reflecting upon our life, we focus on our failures. These failures have the potential to bring us down. It is in these times of reflection we can beat ourselves up and make ourselves feel down, or we can learn by taking appropriate actions to build ourselves up.

Even with failure, we can choose wisdom from this learning while improving in the wake of our mistakes. And how do we go about this improving? Well first of all, we make a choice and stand firm to take committed actions to build ourselves up even after the worst of circumstances. And when we take these positive committed actions, they will allow us to grow from any difficult experience. The fact remains, we will reflect upon these challenging times, we just won't focus on them because the potential of negativity closes our mind, not allowing the possibilities of learning, thus improving and growing from these reflective experiences.

Now that we know a bit more about reflection connection, what are some of the benefits to reflecting? Here are three to get us started:

1. Reflecting Helps You See Yourself

As we reflect, we go deep within to get a clearer vision of who we are. A deeper understanding of our feelings helps us see ourselves. It is when we see ourselves for who we are, that improves our self-awareness. This is that inner drive of *being* that I referred to previously. Self-awareness is essential as we begin our reflective experiences and the possible actions that would result from our thinking time. It shows us the good, the bad, what we should do, and what results we are looking for from our reflective experiences.

2. Reflecting Provides A Deeper Understanding

It is the understanding of our emotions during our reflective experiences that create our feelings. Further, it is our reflective feelings that shape the responses to our experiences. Our inner drive emotions speak to us. This understanding links to the possibilities of the actions we should take regarding our experiences. Our understanding also includes our perspective concerning the reflective experience. This perspective helps us see the contrasts of who we are with who we want to be, and what we are presently doing. It also provides us with the understanding to act upon what we should be doing. Again, it is this *doing* I speak of that is the outer drive actions we take to learn and grow in life.

3. Reflecting Develops Patience

The process begins with our thinking or reflecting upon our experiences. We then move to the beginning of the connecting phase. But it all starts with what we think. Again, I refer to this as – *thinking about what you want to think about*. This focused effort is what I refer to as our inner drive of thoughts. It is vital that for this purposeful process that we remain patient. There is much patience during the reflecting stages from thinking, feeling, and responding to them. All these stages take time to develop. It is not until you complete these crucial stages that the last phase takes place – taking compelling and committed actions to learn and grow from reflective experiences.

Again, be patient. Reflections take time developing into powerful connections with your past, present, and future. The goal in reflection connection is to initiate new perspectives to embrace your life; thus, enriching it toward fulfillment. It is in the process of enrichment that includes our most important actions, leading us to learning and growth, then the continuous fulfillment of this growth leads us to our personal potential.

11

Reflection Connections Happen Within

Reflection connections happen in you. Too many times we are focused only on what happens to us. We forget that we alone direct how we think and feel within. This process of our inner drive keeps us focused and motivated within.

The fact is reflection connections promote self-awareness – and this inner drive of self-awareness enables us to see within ourselves more clearly. It is self-awareness that opens the doors to our mind and hearts that bring enrichment into our lives. Again, reflection connections help us see ourselves for who we really are and a clear view of ourselves is vital for new perspectives regarding where we are to where we desire to go in life. But to go anywhere in life, we must go beyond simply reflecting, and that is only through committed actions.

Going Beyond Reflections Happen on the Outside

We now move this self-awareness and put it to work. This work happens on the outside. Further, this work, or actions lead us to personal growth. But how do we know if we have grown? Growth is only experienced after we take outer drive committed actions. These actions happen on the outside. To ensure growth, we must ask ourselves questions. So, ask yourself: Where have I grown most from my experiences? If you can answer this question with the idea that you have taken certain measures, or actions regarding personal growth, then this is where you will also find most success in life.

Let's stop there for a moment. Now, ask yourself another question: Do I always take needed, appropriate actions according to what I reflect upon? Be honest with regards to this question. Why? Because many of us create self-imposed barriers and obstacles to not follow-through with necessary actions regarding their reflective experiences. (We will discuss overcoming barriers and obstacles throughout the book.) Yes. This is where many of us fail. It is not just any response but taking the appropriate actions that we know will help us grow after we have reflected upon our experiences in life. Maybe the word 'fail' is too harsh for most of us to hear, but the unfortunate truth is that many of us don't take the necessary actions after we reflect to grow from our experiences.

There is good news. We can change this unfortunate fact and turn our responses into actions, thus learn and grow from them. Because true personal growth is continuous. The key to continuous growth is to stay hungry. And this my friends, is the idea behind personal potential. Again, as I discussed in the introduction, that I refer to our potential as 'personal'. Because we are all unique. We all have a different potential, personal to us, only to us as individuals. That's what makes this book important to you, only you. It's personal.

Never stop growing! To stay hungry, we must focus our attention on reflecting each day. Our attitude, character, passion, and purpose are all a part of enhancing and growing in life. When we take the time to reflect on our lives – the ups and downs, joys and disappointments – we learn more about ourselves. When we emerge from this learning upon our past and our present-day experiences, we then discover a new appreciation of who we are and the life we lead today and where we want to go into the future.

Purposeful Growth

This growth I refer to just doesn't happen all the sudden. In other words, growth is not automatic – you must be purposeful about it. If you don't try to improve yourself each day, your growth stays in the same place – thus, you will be stuck where you are today, doing the same things and hoping for the same hopes. Hopes and dreams are just that, they are intentions without actions. Improving yourself requires committed actions.

Focused reflections allow us to ask ourselves the question: What's next? And it also consists of a difference between thoughts and actions. Thinking about growth is a good beginning, but it is only when you take the necessary actions that growth actually starts. Growing is the result of experiencing new things or actions we take in life. The day we stop growing is the day we forfeit our individual personal potential in life.

The only way to grow in life is to be purposeful about it. Two words: Growth matters. *"Can't teach an old dog new tricks"* – I am not sure where that statement came from, but many of us humans have the same mentality! I have discovered that life is a journey of learning and growing, and if you are purposeful about it, you will always enhance your life. But remember, intentions are only the beginning of the process. Our intentions act as our inner drive that speak to us. It is only when we take committed outer drive actions that we realize our enhanced life. I honestly believe part of our meaning and purpose is to look at our life as a continuous effort to enhance it.

And that my friends, will be the focus of this book. Purposefully creating action steps from our reflective experiences to first, learn, then grow from, and finally leading us to unlimited personal potential.

CHAPTER 2

WHAT IS BEYOND REFLECTING?

So, beyond reflecting, what does that really mean? First of all, reflecting is a more purposeful way of thinking. I believe most of us, when we focus upon some particular thing, event, or situation that we are doing it in a purposeful way. In reflection, we flow through our thoughts to feelings, then a response. Responses are anything from asking ourselves a question – What should I do? – to – doing nothing, and leaving our current thoughts and feelings, moving on to the next reflection. Yes. Responses can be nothing more, nothing less.

Don't we all need, and want more in life? I would say – yes. We certainly need more in life if we want to experience increased learning and growing opportunities toward our personal potential. To go beyond reflecting upon any experience; what we need are results. With results, there is concrete evidence of completion. Where there are results, there is also learning and growth.

Results. Why is there even a need for results? And if there is a need for a result, then what must we do? Unfortunately, these questions usually go unanswered. Many of us believe that a result is just another thought of 'what could be'. Or maybe it's an emotion or two, but it really doesn't go anywhere. But shouldn't we all want more from life than just our thoughts and feelings? Let's answer the two other questions before moving on. First, the question of why a need for a result after we reflect upon an experience? Well, as I stated, it is the result that creates learning and growth. Secondly, the question of what must we do to attain this result? In this case, the only way to experience a result from a reflective experience, is through demonstrated actions.

Now, don't you want more from your thoughts and feelings after you have reflected upon them? If the answer is – yes, then this book is for you! And even if you're not sure, keep reading, you will discover some things that may change your life. But also understand this – to go from actions to personal potential as the subtitle of this book suggests, will take some work. Well, a lot of work, but well worth your efforts!

Let's go back to results. Have you ever wondered why so much of life is unfinished business? That is because it is the result that should be accounted for by an action attached to complete the purposeful thought, or reflection. Okay, stop there. Note, I stated 'should'. Why? Because that is where many of us remain. Knowing we should do something, but not following through with an action to experience the result – which many times, provides us with growth. Yes. Unfortunately, that's where many of us fall short, and that is taking the necessary actions from our reflective experiences to provide learning, and by the way, personal growth from them.

In my previous book – *The Reflection Connection – Reflecting and Connecting to Life's Experiences*, I shared the process of thinking, feeling, and responding to our reflections. In this book, we will start where we left off – going one step further to personal potential. The only way to move closer to personal potential is through a process of taking necessary actions, that lead to learning, then growth, and finally self-improvement. It is only through this process that brings us closer to our personal potential.

What about Potential?

Fact: We will never reach our full potential. What? Wait. We have all been told to 'work toward our full potential'. So, what's the problem? Well, the problem is that some of us believed that once we attained this 'full potential', (so, we thought) we have reached the pinnacle of life. Remember, we touched upon this in the introduction of this book. Let's look at yet another perspective. If we believe that we have reached the pinnacle of life, then we have convinced ourselves that there are no more needs concerning efforts, no more learning, and no more growth. This couldn't be more wrong! Life is meant to be a never-ending journey of continuous learning and growing! The wonderful part about this truth is that we have the opportunity to keep moving forward through reflecting upon daily experiences to grow from them. It is when we grow from any experience that we move toward our personal potential.

Note – 'toward' – moving forward, continually striving for our own personal potential. As we have discussed, then why do we term it as personal potential? It's because we are all unique as to what we deem as 'our' potential. Think about that for a moment. It's considered 'our' potential – ours alone. It is our *inner-most being* where our own individual personal potential lies. Making it personal to just you, and there is no pressure, no limits but what you put upon yourself. What we have then is complete ownership of our own growth. But, also know this, we all have untapped potential that is just waiting to express itself to you and the world! It is the material in this book that will take you on a journey that goes beyond simply responding to your reflections but, much further in creating intentional actions that will lead to enhanced learning and growth which moves us closer to our personal potential.

I will be with you along the way sharing common life examples that will go beyond merely reflecting regarding our life's experiences, but to provide you with proven methods, techniques, and principles that lead to actions. These actions will then inspire your learning toward the next level – personal growth. And it is this personal growth that leads you to maximizing self-improvements moving you closer to your own individual potential.

These concepts will go beyond the simple responses to reflections moving you to growth. The responses from the first book: *The Reflection Connection* regarding purposeful reflections were only meant to provide better self-awareness. It is your self-awareness which provides a great foundation toward moving you to the next stage regarding your reflective experiences. That next stage is taking compelling and committed actions from these experiences to learn and grow, which provides the foundation to your personal potential.

This book and its contents will take you on a journey filled with the necessary actions regarding learning, growing, and personal potential. And after we take necessary actions, this learning and growth is then realized. Once we recognize growth, we also experience self-improvements. But also know this, we will need to take specific steps to reach any attainment of personal potential.

Along with the common examples I will share, I also would imagine that many of you will most likely want to respond with your own unique actions. Remember, they are yours – it's personal. I may provide you with examples, but you will want to respond with your own, personal acts that you would want to take. That's the beauty. Think of it this way – I provide the roadmap; you are in the driver's seat. Understanding this need for your own responses, I will provide effective steps, methods, principles, and techniques along the way to inspire your own behaviors to move you toward growth after reading these examples.

The Value of Actions

For a moment, let's go back to the idea of knowing we should act, but remain disengaged. What about the value of our actions? Remember, it begins with our reflections. In reflecting, many people do not recognize the value that once they have reflected on thoughts and feelings regarding their experiences, that they just let them go without doing anything about them. In other words, through reflecting upon experiences you had, and even recognizing there is a good lesson from them; yet doing nothing with them. If your reflections stop at thoughts of action, and you advance no further, then you remain where you started – just your thoughts. And the consequences of not following through with a response, hence no growth from the experience. The true value of intentional reflecting is to respond with committed actions after you have deeply thought about the potential learning that comes from both past and present experiences. With learning comes growth. When you respond with authority to take the first step toward necessary actions to grow, you improve your life.

When intentionally reflecting, you must understand that every thought and feeling has the potential to go to the next level of committed actions and be applied in a way that growth can be maximized. Intentional responses start with questions. In reflecting, the thoughts go from asking yourself the first question of – What must I do? This is your plan of action. This question should be instinctive because it is the foundation that is followed by – If I take appropriate action, is there something I can learn from this experience? – in addition to – What is the possibility of growth that I can gain from this experience? Then, maybe the most important question: What impact did my actions have on the results of the possibilities of learning and growing from my reflective experience? The value of taking appropriate actions after reflecting becomes the foundation for personal potential.

How to Turn Responses into Growth

So, how do we turn simple responses into growth? As you read in the first chapter, it is purposeful reflection connections that allow us to expand upon a deeper sense of introspection in shaping our thoughts, inspiring and stretching our feelings, and initiating natural responses to promote better self-awareness. If we go beyond reflecting, this improved self-awareness is then embraced with committed actions and applied to learning, that then leads us to personal growth which in turn produces enrichment in our lives. Note: 'If'. That's where this book comes in. This book, and its contents replaces the 'if' with undeniable actions to produce substantial growth enhancements in our life.

So, Why Not Go One Step Further?

We can call it growth, self-improvement, lessons learned – they all lead to one thing – personal potential. We should always be improving ourselves toward our potential in life. For the theme of this book, we will focus upon how actions lead to growth, therefore moving us to our own individual personal potential.

It is learning that unlocks your self-improvement. And it is self-improvement that moves you from how good you currently are, to how great you could be. In other words, embracing learning and the pure act of self-improvement goes deeper, or one step further, to complete the connection to your reflections. Again, my previous book focused upon our purposeful thoughts and feelings; immediately followed by responses to become more self-aware.

Having intentional thoughts and feelings while reflecting is only the start of the self-awareness process. It is the effective actions you take after your reflections that learning and growth begin to take shape. Growth begins with actions. It is these actions that will lead you to your own personal potential.

Before actions take shape, we must reflect upon intentional questions that will provide us the motivation to keep focused so that the actions on the outside result in growth. Why? Because there is a gap before growth arrives. That gap is learning. Once the learning is applied, growth blossoms. Now we can move to self-improvements and finally, to personal potential. Let's go back to the idea of gaps for a moment. Remember that the process is also filled with barriers and obstacles to deal with. Again, let me be clear, the path to striving for personal potential requires challenging work to result in any successes that you experience.

It will be the compelling and committed actions that will lead us to our personal potential, but only through a journey of the process that moves us there.

Here are some questions to get us started:

1. Now that you have reflected upon your experience, what's next?

(*Chapter 3 – Start and End with Thoughts*)

2. Are there possible barriers to taking the next steps of acting upon my reflective experience?

(*Chapter 4 – Combating Barriers to Act*)

3. What are the actions I must take regarding my reflective experience?

(*Chapter 5 & 6 – Call's to Action, and then Chapter 7 – Time for Action*)

4. Are there steps I must take to capitalize on learning and growing from necessary actions regarding my reflective experience?

(*Chapter 8 and Chapter 9 – Learning Leads to Growth – Part 1 and 2*)

5. After taking the appropriate actions and applying them to learning from my experience, is growth automatic?

(*Chapter 10 – Obstacles to Growth, Chapter 11 – Growth is a Choice, Chapter 12 – Steps to Growth*)

6. As I grow, what does that do for my self-improvement endeavors?

(*Chapter 13 – Self-Improvement Leads to Growth*)

7. Are there things I can do to maximize my personal potential?

(*Chapter 14 – Action Potential, Chapter 15 – Actions and Your Personal Potential*)

These questions will be addressed as we move through the book. You will note that I added the related chapters to each question. As you read through the chapters, one leads to the other in a process that will keep you moving from beyond reflecting to taking actions leading you to your personal potential. Of course, as in life, there will be barriers and obstacles along the way we will need to address and understand to get to the next step in the process.

First learning, then growth is applied to move us closer to our personal potential. If you are like most, the responses to reflections will seem almost automatic, or natural. Learning starts with responding. Responding is the foundation to connecting to our life's experiences. But to have a complete connection that will provide growth, action is essential.

So, in this book, we will go beyond simply responding to our reflective experiences to taking effective actions that initiate growing and move us toward our own personal potential.

In reflecting, many people do not recognize the value that once they have reflected upon thoughts and feelings regarding their experiences, they must go further into reflection to create effective actions. Not understanding this wonderful opportunity and potential for personal growth is unfortunate. So, in other words, it's knowing there is action needed, yet ignoring our thoughts and feelings with no response which leads to complications, regret, and by the way, no growth. Another way to think about it is that although reflecting upon life experiences, and maybe even recognizing some of the potential benefits, many people don't go any further to realize the true lessons within these experiences. This, of course, resulting in no follow-through with actions to actually grow from the reflective experiences. Who wants to live under those conditions? I don't, and I certainly do not believe you want this kind of life without enhanced learning, nor growth, to strive for your own personal potential.

The true value of reflection connections is to take actions after you have deeply thought about the potential learning that come from past and present experiences. With learning comes self-improvement, then growth; thus, increasing your personal potential.

When purposefully reflecting, you must understand that every thought and feeling has the possibility to go to the next level of taking appropriate actions that will lead you to your own personal potential.

Read on ...

CHAPTER 3

START AND END WITH THOUGHTS

Everything begins and ends with our thoughts. The beginning starts with a simple notion. This notion becomes the gathering of thoughts regarding what we think, the way in which we think, and how we think. The ending thoughts are created as part of the follow-up process after the actions have taken place.

In this chapter, we will focus on the *what,* or the subject of our reflective experience, and the *way,* or approach of our experience. Finally, the *how,* or the attitude we use during our thought process that leads to the necessary actions according to the reflective experience that occurred.

Although not our focus, let me touch upon the end thoughts just as so you get an idea of how we start and end with our thought process as it relates to our reflective experiences. So, the ending thoughts of completed actions start with questions. In reflections, the thoughts go from asking yourself questions of – 'Is there something to learn from this experience?' to 'What is the possible growth that I can gain from this experience?' These action-oriented thoughts grow to feelings of 'What to do'. We will go into greater detail regarding the ending thought process in the later chapters, but for now, let's focus on *what,* *why,* and *how* our thoughts are used as we enter into the reflective experience.

What You Think Leads to What Actions You Will Take

We start with what you think because what we think defines the experience and what it means to us. Our thoughts become reality if we believe those thoughts to be true. The quality of our thoughts reflects the quality of our life. So, what we think has a lot to do with this reality. Thus, if we were to raise the quality of our thoughts, we would automatically improve the quality of our actions. Our thoughts and how we use them determines what we say and do each day. So, what we think becomes critical when we begin our reflection. Our thoughts, and what we ponder, create how we feel about ourselves and the world around us. It is first our thoughts, then feeling, becomes the foundation to responding with the appropriate actions needed.

What we think of any experience is also a reflection of ourselves. For instance, have you ever reflected upon the phrase that goes something like ... *it is all about who we say we are?* This one phrase starts with what we think. It is because what we think defines who we truly are. The way in which we reflect and what we think are completely under our direction. Where our mind goes, we follow – we become what we think. What we think and reflect upon determines our day and how we live it.

What You Think is What YOU Think

As you reflect, ask yourself ... Who directs my mind? The answer is you. Do not let the outside world direct it – do not allow others to influence you regarding what you want to think about yourself.

It is important to stress that you are in control of your own individual thoughts while reflecting – they are in fact, your corner of freedom. No one can tell you what or how to think. The key is to not allow others to influence your values and what you think. Remember that we are all unique which also means we all will think differently while taking part in reflection. These reflective thoughts are what lead us to action.

Reflections upon our thoughts become feelings, and these feelings determine how we act. In reflection we can change what we think and, in turn change our feelings and thus, altering our actions. In other words, we direct our thoughts, feelings, and actions as they unfold regarding each experience.

People believe events cause what we feel. These feelings are a natural response – automatic – then you choose what to do with them. But it is first what we think, then it is telling ourselves about these events that initiates how we will respond. It is from both our thoughts and feelings that are vital tools when reflecting upon life's experiences. Without these tools, we cannot complete the actions after the reflective experiences.

We direct our own reflections and what we think – not from some outside source. Unfortunately, there are those who are conditioned to think narrow-minded thoughts and are controlled by or strongly influenced to think like others they spend most of their time with. This is no way to live life. Again, what we think determines how we live our lives. It is our responsibility to take charge of our own life.

It is vital to be in control of your thoughts as you begin your reflections. With this focus, it will determine where you go with your thoughts regarding your reflection, and therefore establish how you will respond with actions. With control of your thoughts, it also means that you can experience positive thoughts while reflecting; thus, resulting in positive outcomes to your actions.

The Way You Think Leads You to How You Think
Reflective experiences begins with what we think, then moves to the way in which we think. The way in which we think makes a crucial

difference in how we approach the necessary actions we must take.

After we decide what we think, next is then how we approach our thoughts. Just as what we think about has its own importance, it is the way in which we think that creates our viewpoints throughout the day. And it is these viewpoints that move us to how we think, or the attitudes that will lead us in taking actions from our reflective experiences. When we begin to reflect, we establish how our approach will affect our perspective or viewpoint. These viewpoints then become the way in which we think. And it will be these viewpoints that determine how you will think regarding the course of actions from the reflection.

Reflecting and living life internally is your responsibility. It starts with what you think. Again, it's important to understand – first what you think, then secondly is the way in which you think, then lastly, how you think about the experience that will determine what actions you will take.

Taking responsibility in living happily and effectively, is a choice we all make or don't. The emotions of being happy are feelings that are created by the way in which we think, and how our thoughts are decided. The ability to think and reflect in a positive manner, then respond with control and take charge of our life lies within us. A productive life is about taking responsibility for our thoughts, feelings, and actions.

Our life's journey is full of events; good and bad. We have no control over most events, but we do have control over the way we think and how we respond to all events through our reflections.

An action after any reflection is initiated from the foundation created by our thoughts. The way in which we think is the understanding that we cannot always choose what happens around us, what happens to us; but we can always choose what happens within us.

In other words, some things in life are beyond our control and it is up to us to choose the way we want to think about these things and how we will respond within.

Intuition is the Thought Before the Action

Yet another way to think is intuitively, or as I refer to it as *intuitive thoughts*. It is our intuition that provides our thoughts with the fuel to begin our action plan. Intuition is that feeling, or emotion that you get just before something is about to happen. These instinctive feelings provide us with an emotional foundation to make decisions based on our intuition. Although all reflections begin with our thoughts, it is feelings that follow. Once this process is complete, actions are necessary for learning and growing opportunities.

Reflection allows us to be intuitive regarding our thinking abilities, which then affects our actions we take. We have all used our intuition from time to time – it bypasses for the most part, critical thinking or analyzing in making decisions. In other words, it is our intuition that is based on more of a 'gut feeling.' In reflection, we may go quickly from the thinking to the feeling phase. Intuition originates from this gut feeling that connects to our own self-truth. When we reflect, intuition is imaginative and many times surprising. With intuition, we receive an emotional sense before thinking and reflecting about it. In this case, strong feelings come before concentrated thinking. This is why I refer to them as intuitive thoughts.

A 'Will Do' Attitude Leads to Effective Actions

We have reviewed what we think and the way we think – both vitally important, but it is how you think that determines your attitude. And it will be this attitude of choice that will lead us to the important actions that result from our reflective experiences. An attitude of *will do* will go much further in life than an attitude focused on *maybe someday I will get around to it* thought process. Remember, previously we discussed the issue regarding thoughts of 'unfinished business' and our frustration concerning this subject. The idea of *getting around to it* is just that. Meaning, although we recognize our need to take appropriate actions, we delay. Why? We make excuses for not following-through. The only way to move beyond this excuse is to change our attitude.

This idea of delaying actions requires us to change. We must first change our thoughts. In other words, we change our thoughts from – *it can wait* – to – *do it now*. Further, reflecting upon necessary changes in our lives requires a *will do* attitude if we want to encounter effective actions regarding life experiences.

If we want to change something, we must be intentional about it. We must want to do it. We all can want change, but it begins with what we think before choosing an attitude regarding how we think. This is an attitude in which we change how we think from *would* or *should* – to a positive attitude of *will do*. Why? Because the words *would* and *should* are only unproductive thoughts and short-lived feelings regarding reflective experiences whereas thoughts of *will do* leads to committed actions to move closer to completion and success regarding the reflective experiences you encounter.

Think Possibilities

It is how we think that consumes our attitudes as we enter important decisions concerning our actions. For example, those that seem to have more of a negative attitude will many times think and reflect upon the obstacles in their path rather than to look at the possibilities first. It is only by focusing and reflecting upon a brighter future that begins a positive outlook regarding the actions to be taken. Without reflecting upon the possibilities first, we struggle to see our true potential in the things we want in life because we do not look beyond the obstacles in front of us.

Endless reflective thoughts of possibilities are transformed into feelings of abundance, of no barriers, and nothing less than continuous actions in life. Even the word – endless – evokes a thought process of no limits regarding the actions we can take. With thoughts and reflections such as this, we can create positive thoughts and reach for higher levels of personal growth. By starting with the possibilities, we can then begin to see the potential in knowing we can attain what we really want in life. Only we have the control; we alone can remove the self-imposed obstacles that stop us from moving forward toward the endless possibilities life has for us.

But remember that endless possibilities only start with how we think – our attitude. If we are to create a life of endless possibilities, we must then focus upon what are the potentials of the experience we choose to reflect upon. Remember that before any successful results in our reflective experiences can be realized, our attitude must be right with positive thoughts and openness for all things that life presents us. With this kind of attitude, all possibilities are attainable through our reflective experiences, thus taking the necessary actions to be successful.

Attitudes Are Everything as We Think

As we enter our reflective experiences, there are many times we find ourselves focusing on *what happened* versus *next time*. In life, what happened is already in the past and there is nothing we can do to change it. What is worse is if the *what happened* ended in a negative consequence. With negative consequences come the feeling of failure. These doubtful emotions create reflections that are focused on *only if* scenarios that cannot be changed. In this case, people believe that they are locked into negative consequences during reflection and go into situations set up to fail as they push forward in their attempts to take necessary actions.

Or how about playing the victim regarding our reflective experiences? It comes down to how you think. Those that stay thinking that their life is beyond control are only victims of their own reality. Then there are those that take responsibility for their lives and create positive thinking that embraces positive choices regarding the actions they will take. Those that think in this way have a much better chance toward creating a positive attitude regarding their circumstances. How we think and respond with action is completely under our own guidance. Our attitude and how we respond with actions is the difference. So, really it truly comes down to how we think.

How we think consists of many emotions including happy or sad, positive or negative – we choose. It is important to understand that we alone choose our attitudes and not from some outside source. It comes from within.

The opportunity to connect becomes possible after we give much thought to our choices of reflective experiences regarding what and the way in which we think, and how we think then leads us to the actions we take according to those experiences.

The secret is to never feel locked into anything that you can change. As we are in reflection, even if the experience was negative and did not end well, there are positive outcomes of actions that can result from the overall experience. These positive outcomes regarding actions we experience, are learning lessons. It is these positive lessons that can alter your future regarding the next similar reflective experience.

Further, with positive lessons in place, there can always be valuable learning, new awareness, or understanding even in the worst of circumstances. The most important lesson is not to be locked into anything that you can change. There is nothing more invigorating than understanding that you are not locked into a particular way of thinking and reflecting – it is a choice. With a will-do attitude, you can change anything you set out to do. It is a comforting feeling to discover that the circumstances of today can be changed into something new and positive tomorrow.

The beauty of this feeling is that it can be easily achieved by just reflecting upon thinking differently – and in doing so, seeing the world differently with any attitude that you choose. By changing our mind-set to *the next time it is going to be right* is one with a *will do* attitude. This is the understanding that we have direction over how we think and respond with actions to all of life's situations. We must always remember that the situation itself does not dictate our feelings; it is what we tell ourselves about the event that determines it.

New Thinking Leads to Growth

There is nothing like the excitement of something new. That goes for our thinking abilities as well. Without new reflective thoughts, the same, unchanged beliefs will only keep you from moving forward in life. Reflective experiences allow us to create opportunities to think new thoughts resulting in improving our lives through effective actions.

All reflections begin with our thoughts regarding the life experiences we choose. Because our reflections start with thoughts, it is also important to be open to new perspectives regarding the subject matter of these reflections. By thinking the same pattern of thoughts, change, nor actions cannot occur. In other words, the outcome is the same results. In addition, with the use of this continuous pattern of unchanged thoughts, there is no growth. Without change, there is no incentive to enhance our life. The results are that we and our life remain stagnant. If we focus our reflections on the old ways of thinking, we do not allow change to enter, nor do we explore new paths as we are initiating actions.

It makes a lot of sense, but how many of us stick to the old ways of doing things because it has always worked for us in the past? Or even worse, we continue doing the same things (old ways) and expecting a different result. The result is limited personal growth, no new thinking possibilities. Just take a moment and truly contemplate if we did things differently how much more fulfillment and potential we could attain from every situation or event we experience.

A lesson for all of us – young and old, it is never too late to change our reflections regarding what, our way of, and how we think. We should always be searching and striving to reach personal potential in life. This is only possible if we think of new and innovative ways to do things. This begins through our reflections regarding each experience as it unfolds. The result is the opportunity to learn, grow, and enrich our life. The question then is how to move from the old to the new?

How to move from old to new is through reflection creativity. We all can use more imagination, be more inventive, and bring things to a new light in our lives – making life more exciting and adventurous. With new, creative ways of thinking will also lead us to creative actions from these reflective experiences. It all starts with new thinking. This new thinking is then integrated into our reflective experiences moving us toward action-oriented opportunities to improve our lives. If we focus on creative alternatives regarding our innovative thoughts and ideas, we will then see the world differently, which in turn, we will undergo more effective actions from our reflective experiences to learn and grow, and always striving for our personal potential.

In this chapter, the focus was a journey through the thought process of what we think in defining our reflective experience, the way in which we think, or the approach we will take, and finally, how we think regarding the experience and the attitudes that carry us through to shape our actions. And many times, the results? New, creative thinking for the best possible, compelling, and committed actions.

CHAPTER 4

COMBATING BARRIERS TO ACT

Let's be honest. When we really get to the truth regarding our barriers to act, all we must do is look in the mirror. Yes. We are the barrier in most instances regarding why we don't proceed after we reflect. This notion to proceed I speak of is the undeniable, compelling evidence to take required actions from our life's experiences. Now, think about how many times you moved on to some other thought; consciously leaving a reflective experience that you knew needed action. And that's what I am referring to. We become the barrier to taking the required actions that move us forward to learn and grow in striving for our personal potential.

These barriers are common to all of us, at various levels, but they all affect us at one time or another. Besides various levels, barriers come in varied excuses as well. Yes. I stated excuses. Remember, in many cases, we are the barrier. Here are some common ones for many of us: limited thinking, fear, making assumptions, and possibilities of failure. We will discuss these barriers and what we have in common with, and how we need to use trust within ourselves to combat them. In addition, how the value of taking responsibility will also assist in resolving our barriers to act upon our reflective experiences so that we can in turn learn, grow, and strive for our personal potential.

Limited Thinking

What if I were to tell you that most studies state on average, we only use a low percentage of our thinking abilities? I also think that many of us would have a challenging time believing it. The truth is we all have much more capacity available to us. The question would be why we don't act upon attaining advanced knowledge, learn more skills, or enhance our natural talents? Unfortunately, the answer for many of us is we get complacent, we get lazy, we even stop wanting to go further in life. What's in the way of enhancing our life? Sadly, it's us. It is the same thing regarding our required notions to act. We create limited thinking surrounding reflective experiences and do not take appropriate actions. What's holding us back? Remember, it all begins with our thoughts. It is what and how we think that create these barriers to act.

In the previous chapter we discussed how our thoughts begin and end regarding our reflective experiences, but if we impede these thoughts at the beginning of the process, we remain with that barrier. It is also possible that we can improve this statement by concentrating deeply upon action-oriented thoughts while reflecting. These action-oriented thoughts go beyond mere intentions to act, but to ensure that we physically carry them out. But first, we must put into our mind compelling reasons to act. Compelling reasons to act you say? Yes, it is with deep and focused thoughts, that we also go beyond touching the surface of limited thoughts to the powerful wisdom that we can discover by thinking outside our limitations. The key to success is unlocking this untapped wisdom and accessing these abilities to reach for what we really want, and that is enhanced learning and growing potential.

Let's go back to our barriers for a moment. If everything starts with our thoughts, then if we limit those thoughts, we also remain right there – with limited thinking. When we reflect with limited thinking it can lead to a narrow view of life and reduce any chances of possible actions regarding our experiences. Limited thinking defines those that do not look for, or even to refuse to be open to innovative ideas, opinions, or perspectives concerning a reflective experience that requires actions to grow.

All too often we limit our thinking. This is especially true when we face difficult challenges in life. Why? Because it's easier for most to just give in or give up regarding the difficult challenges put before them. It's not because we can't resolve them, but that we purposely limit ourselves and our abilities to take actions that we know and understand are necessary according to the experience we have reflected upon.

Many of us get so concerned that we will never overcome our challenges, nor will we ever accomplish what we set out to do. Thoughts such as these will only limit our greater growth potential.

Unfortunately, there are many that think this way, but it is this type of thinking that limits our perspective. If we get programmed into thinking and reflecting that we have limited abilities; once programmed, we then are conditioned to limited thinking and remain in the same place with negative consequences of limited results. Conditioned by this type of limited thinking, we then quit trying and at times, even withdraw and develop thoughts of expecting we will have limitations. Having thoughts such as this, will only hamper any possible actions while reflecting upon an experience that requires us to take these necessary actions.

Effective reflective actions requires positive focus and extra effort. This kind of effort means to exert energy, and if used effectively, it can be put to good use for continuous growth through your reflective actions. A positive focus and exerting energy are on emotional and physical levels. It's unfortunate that many are not willing to put in the work to move from less than average to the best they can be.

This is exactly why your thoughts while reflecting should not be affected by limited thinking, but to believe in yourself and your endless abilities to take necessary actions. Making full use of your abilities is the self-confidence in commanding the direction regarding your level of effort and your life. It is people with extra effort that are in the driver's seat. (Remember previously, I stated that I would provide the roadmap, but you are in the driver's seat regarding the actions you need to take.) They know what it takes to get ahead in life, and they act upon it with energy, confidence, pride, and passion. This kind of extraordinary effort is discovered when you think you are done but keep going to complete effective and productive actions regarding your reflections.

Our minds can expand with effort. This effort begins with what and how we think. If it is true that the average person is using a low percentage of their thinking abilities, then we already know there is room for growth. Never go a day without reflecting upon unlimited thinking regarding how you can learn more about yourself and make positive differences in your life right now. The truth is that you can do anything that you put your mind to, if only you want it intensely enough. There are no real limits except the limits you place upon yourself. It is only self-limiting beliefs, which are under your control, that hold you back.

Limitations are Common Obstacles

Let's go further into obstacles and why they may limit us in life. As we just reflected upon some self-imposed obstacles regarding limited thinking and how they can affect us, one of the most common obstacles is the one we place upon ourselves, and that is limitations regarding our abilities. When we reflect upon our limitations as obstacles, they can also be damaging. The truth is that most of us have unlimited potential that we don't even know we have.

The damaging effect of reflecting focused upon our limitations have the potential to stop us from moving forward to grow in life. While reflecting, we will at times limit ourselves in thinking that our abilities are not capable of being what we want them to be. But we must remain focused upon our confidence within because it is our abilities that are the key components of striving for our personal potential. It is when we reflect upon thinking our abilities are at a low level of limitations that stop us from effectively living our life.

Is there some kind of special key to success moving beyond our limitations? There is no special key! It is simply what we think, and we can change what we think. It is when we reflect regarding limitations that we can create self-doubt. So, if limitations are self-created then we simply can change how we think. Our abilities go way beyond our reflections. The truth is, we never know how far we can go until our limits are tested. The only limitations we possess are the limitations we place upon ourselves.

For example, when most of us reflect upon personal limitations, learning capabilities come to mind. Our learning capabilities define our level of aptitude – our level of knowledge and our growth potential. The question to ask yourselves while reflecting – is there a limitation regarding gaining continuous knowledge? The answer is – no. Only if we allow this limitation will it affect us.

Possibility of Failure
It is the possibility of failure that holds back many people. So, failing. How does that work regarding combating barriers to grow? It is when we realize that failure is actually good for us that we then understand

that it is the results of failure where we grow the most. In fact, failure is our greatest teacher. In other words, we must fail to grow. The only way to grow quickly is to fail early and often.

What, you have never failed at something? You're kidding yourself if you think this way. We all fail. It's an important part of everyone's life's journey. The wonderful thing, the positive thing about failure is that it presents us the wonderful opportunity to learn and grow. So much so that even the process of achievement comes through repeated failures and the constant struggles to move forward regarding actions. This process makes us wiser, stronger, and moves us forward to our personal potential. The fact is, failures should be a regular part of your life. Why? Again, it is because this is the best opportunity to expand. So, in this case, we are allowing ourselves to fail.

But here's the problem – many of us try to stay away from possible errors because of self-negativity that we believe after we make a mistake. Now, the barrier of failure stands firm, holding us in position and not allowing us to move forward. These barriers can be simply resolved by not allowing your failures to affect you negatively. How? By thinking differently. Thinking positive and looking at failures as the opportunity to learn and grow from is the key to moving forward. If you honestly think about your failures, you will discover at least one positive thing resulted because of each one of these mishaps.

Gaining Adversity

Another subset of failure is adversity. Adversity and failure are often the results from many of our first attempts regarding actions. Both adversity and failure should be expected in the process of succeeding, and they also should be viewed as critical parts of it. It is adversity that prompts a person to rethink the status quo. So, if you want to succeed, you will want to adjust along the way. Change your thinking. Change your actions. The average person that makes a mistake will sometimes think of failure. If you change your thinking to 'just another opportunity', you will view the mistake as a learning opportunity to grow.

Fear Can Stop Us in Our Tracks

Most of us are familiar with the acronym of FEAR: it stands for False Experiences Appearing Real. Let's look at this acronym two different ways: False Experiences and two, Appearing Real. False Experiences are the fears we feel. Appearing Real are really just assumptions.

Now ask yourself – how many times have you delayed an action; that you knew was needed as a result of a reflective experience because you were afraid to take that action? Many of us have. May it be that we are fearful, we assume the worst, not confident or trust in our abilities, we have anxiety, or afraid to take a risk. These are all self-imposed barriers.

We will tackle fear first. So, utterly false experiences are not based on reality, but upon our imagination. When you think about it, 99 percent of the things we worry about never come to pass. If this is true, then if we act upon our reflective experiences that we are fearful of, and take actions regardless, fear then eventually loses all its power.

What if we move toward our fears? Confronting our fears also deals with the fear, and once dealt with, you remove it. Makes perfect sense. When you move toward something that you fear, the fear then diminishes in size and influence, becoming smaller and smaller, and eventually it has no influence over your thoughts nor emotions.

Let's look at anxiety. Anxiety is a function of fear but having anxiety can be a good thing. What? I believe most of us tend to hear the word anxiety and think of it as negative. Remember, a negative thought brings about a negative feeling, which then responds as negative. What do we do? We change our thoughts. If you think of anxiety as a negative it can make you believe it is a barrier.

What if we were to think of the word anxiety as being a positive thing? Instead of worry and nervousness think of it as excitement and possibilities! Now, think positive.

Making Assumptions

As in the second part of the acronym of FEAR, Appearing Real is assuming. One common area of barriers that can affect us are really not barriers at all. They are called assumptions. It is when we assume things that we get into trouble. In other words, we are just *making stuff up*. As it relates to our reflective experiences, making assumptions of the possible outcomes before we take actions can be dangerous. Maybe it's from past experiences, or from the influence of another person, but assumptions before an action can lead to a failed opportunity of growth.

Unfortunately, we sometimes attach assumptions to our planned actions and fail to complete them at all. Making assumptions are fitting examples of how we allow our own thoughts to get the best of us. It is when we assume that we are already convinced that any unfortunate situation is going to be negative. It is when we make these assumptions about someone or something that we feel the need to take it upon ourselves to create our own negative reality. A so-called negative reality will cloud any forward progress without further identifying the bigger picture of putting more thought into reflecting away from negativity before making reactionary decisions based only upon our assumptions.

The truly unfortunate thing regarding assumptions is that some of us start to believe that these assumptions are real and they become our own reality that then become a negative cycle in our lives. In other words, one assumption leads to another, then another, and so on. The results are that we get lost and don't see a true vision of the world around us. At this point, we get locked into creating assumptions; thus, making our lives more stressful and complicated.

Why is this? Simple. It's because our thoughts are negative, and we believe the worst is going to happen. These are assumptions just the same. There are two basic types of thinking. One is negative thinking; the other is positive thinking. If we habitually send out negative thoughts into the world around us, into our personal world, into our reflective experiences, we then will tend to draw back negative results to ourselves. Thoughts spoken, or even unspoken, possess strong influences. In fact, these influences set forces in action which, inevitably, produce outcomes precisely as conceived, and confirmed. This confirmation would be considered our own negative reality. It is these negative things, negative attitudes, and negative mental pictures that will produce struggles in our lives. With assumptions in our mind, our plan to act, then the endeavor itself, will only lead us to confusion and stress; thus, limited learning and growth potential.

Combating These Barriers

To combat our barriers to act, we need both trust and responsibility within ourselves. Why trust and responsibility? Because they lie within our-'self' and we alone control the outcome.

Let's discuss each element and how they work together to combat our barriers so we can move into actions regarding our reflective experiences. But first, let's talk about something before we can put trust in ourselves, or take responsibility. That is – act as if.

One of the keys to developing trust and responsibility is to 'act as if' you already have these qualities within. In other words, you're going to 'act as if' limited thinking, fears, assumptions, and possibilities of failures don't exist. Imagine that you are not afraid to take necessary actions. Think about yourself 'as if' having no limited thinking, no fear, no assumptions, and no possibility of failure existing in whatever reflective experience that may be holding you back from acting upon them.

Next, we want to keep our mind and heart positive. How? It's called positive self-talk. Always speak positively about yourself. Be careful never to say anything about yourself that you do not want to be true. Combating these barriers are not always easy, especially if you have had them within you for an extended period of time. And also, be aware, as you move forward, there will be occasions that you will take a step back in your forward progress, but never criticize yourself nor put yourself down. If you make a mistake, immediately cancel it by saying something like, *next time will be better*.

The key is when you continually speak positive about yourself, these words are soon accepted by your subconscious mind. Next, your subconscious thoughts will then actualize feelings, as well as your actions. Speak to yourself the way that you want to be. Positive and with self-confidence. Think and *act as if* nothing can stop you from learning and growing in life.

Moving Beyond the Barriers

We have now briefly discussed some of the barriers holding us back from acting and some of the things you can do to manage them, but there is no other applicable way you can effectively take actions unless you have trust in yourself and take full responsibility for carrying out required actions from your reflective experiences. Now, armed with our 'act as if' and positive self-talk, let's discuss how trust and responsibility will help you in leaving your barriers behind and how you put *action into your actions*. But, before trust and responsibility, we must choose them.

Barriers of Choice Before Trust and Responsibility

As we must choose trust within ourselves, there are barriers. In addition, we must also choose to take responsibility for our lives. It all begins during our reflections. How we see and understand any situation we experience begins with generating choices to respond to them through our actions. Just choosing to reflect upon each passing day is a choice that we alone make.

Knowingly or not, we make a series of choices all throughout the day. There are good choices and bad, but there are always consequences for each choice we make. There are also consequences for how we choose to reflect upon any situation. These consequences then determine the outcome of the reflections we experience. Any consequences are the result of our actions. These actions are also choices we make. When there are consequences that we believe will affect us in an undesirable way, we many times create self-imposed barriers while in reflection.

If you honestly think about it, life is a succession of choices. More importantly, it's about the type of choices we make. If this is indeed true, then doesn't it make sense to be fully aware of the choices we make? Reflecting upon and taking actions regarding these choices become the consequences for either a successful or just an average reflective experience. You choose.

It is when we choose to put up barriers in front of our progress that get in the way of any potential self-improvements. To know and truly understand just how important each of our choices are; is a vital part of living an effective life. It is only through reflecting upon these choices that we are more aware of our thoughts and feelings to be more effective in life.

What is holding you back from making the right choices? Is it limited thinking? Fear? Assumptions? Or possibility of failure?

Remember, whether it is from any of these excuses, they are the obstacles that stops us from making good choices. There are many self-imposed barriers such as these that we allow to get in the way of taking necessary actions to progress in life. The fact remains that many of these barriers are self-imposed. In other words, what barriers we create regarding our reflections within, then affect us on the outside world.

These same barriers affect who we want to be and where we want to go in life. But think about this – aren't these self-imposed barriers simply choices we are making?

Creating self-imposed barriers regarding choices will only limit our reflection experiences. When we limit our reflective experiences, we also put limits upon learning and growing opportunities. Thus, we must rid ourselves of these negative barriers and think in a positive frame of mind. To connect to a positive point of view, you must start by choosing to think and reflect with a positive attitude. Ever wondered what obstacles hold you back from moving forward in life? Again, I would wager that many of these so-called barriers are self-imposed. We all hold the power to direct our own journey along with the attitude and choices we make. If we are indeed the ones that create these obstacles, then we also possess the ability to unravel them. If we do not use this power to remove our barriers of choices while reflecting, we may miss out on many good things in life because of these obstacles. When you think about it – the barriers of choices we allow, we also accept. These are choices we alone make. So, it sounds simple by not allowing negative barriers, and that's not accepting them as well. It's all about the choices in which we make.

If we understand that it is self-imposed barriers that stops us from living the life we want, then it only makes sense that we need to acknowledge that we also have the power in releasing these barriers through reflecting upon them.

Now, putting trust within yourself and taking the responsibility to make the right choices will also assist you in taking the right actions to learn and grow. Remember, these are simply choices we make. Live the life you were meant to live. Having the freedom to make good choices and work through your barriers that are stopping you from effective reflective experiences, will create the right actions that are necessary after each experience. Now that we have moved beyond the self-imposed barriers, we can put trust in ourselves and take the necessary responsibility to live life effectively.

Trust in Ourselves

Combating barriers to act requires trust within yourself. One way to put trust in yourself is to be confident. In other words, you must trust in your abilities. There are times that trusting our own judgment can affect us in the way in which we live our life. The fact is, we all go through difficult periods of life and at times, the outcomes can affect our self-confidence. When these times are before us, we must learn to always trust in ourselves especially when making decisions and taking actions during troubled circumstances as they relate to our reflective experiences. When we discover the ability to trust in ourselves, we will then know the right thing to do at the right time according to the required actions that must be taken.

Knowingly or not, you are the best person to hold your trust. It is you that truly is equipped and the most experienced – in you. This is exactly why you want to put trust in your heart because it is there that your self-confidence is stored – just waiting for you to put all trust in you. Putting trust in yourself matters because it is within you that accountability and responsibility both lie. It will be this trust, or self-confidence in your abilities that will spell success regarding the actions you take after reflecting upon an experience.

Life is a series of decisions that you alone must be the owner of producing and sorting through. Others may help or influence those decisions, but it is you that faces the consequences of those decisions. As we experience events and situations in life, it is our trust within and self-confidence that we must depend upon.

Trust is also Taking Risks

Our life's journey is full of events; good and bad. Good or bad, we still have the responsibility to act. Let's take risks for example. Good and bad can come from taking risks. How do we know this? Because it has occurred throughout our lives. But what have we learned from taking these risks? We have learned what works and what doesn't. In this learning process, we grow more confident knowing the right decisions are made at the right time. Risk taking is a part of a successful life. I have a saying – *If you're not risking, you're not living*.

Without this trust within, we will not take the necessary risks in life to be successful nor will we take actions that lead to growth. Trusting within ourselves involves confidence and taking risks to move forward in life.

Now that we are choosing to put trust within ourselves, it's time to take the necessary responsibilities to take actions according to our reflective experiences that moves us toward our personal potential.

Taking Responsibility

One of the most important virtues to possess is to be responsible. Anyone that wants to live a successful life must take responsibility in responding to life's events and situations. In other words, life – you need to own it.

Let's continue with this idea of life and that it is full of responsibilities. For example, one common responsibility that many of us struggle with is admitting when we make a mistake. This is especially true when taking actions after our experiences. For instance, when taking some actions, we don't always get it right. Yes. We sometimes initiate the wrong action, and the result is negative, or less than expected outcome.

So, admitting our mistakes after we act is sometimes difficult. Remember, we just discussed failure and for many of us, mistakes equal failure. May it be vanity or embarrassment, we don't always own up regarding our mishaps. In fact, many of us find it easier to blame our circumstances, or even another person for our own mistake. What to do? Simply take responsibility. It is when we take the responsibility for our own mistakes that our credibility and character are positively enhanced. Do not let pride get in the way of your personal responsibilities in life. How you accomplish your personal responsibilities, also defines you as you attempt to take appropriate actions according to your reflective experiences.

Let's go into more detail regarding mistakes. We should always take responsibility for our mistakes. In fact, like failures, mistakes can be great teachers leading us to learning and personal growth. Mistakes can slow your efforts regarding improvement and can also demoralize you if you allow them to. But if you have growth mentality; you will understand that mistakes are there to educate you. How can your mistakes help you make better decisions as they relate to the actions you must take? Let's look at four-steps regarding taking responsibility for your mistakes.

Four-Steps Regarding Taking Responsibility
Step 1. Admit your mistakes. You can't learn as much from a mistake you don't own up to. Denial only makes the mistake you created worse.

Step 2. You need to accept the responsibility. Again, many of us would rather put blame on someone or something.

Step 3. Fix what you can. There are some things you can take action to lessen the damage, take corrective steps, or if someone is involved, make apologies if the mistake has affected them. If so, do these actions quickly.

Step 4. Lastly, and most importantly, learn from your mistakes. It is when you learn by mistakes, you also grow.

As you continue to read, you will discover that reflective experiences, actions taken, barriers and obstacles identified and resolved, learning, growing, and self-improvement, all contribute to lead you to your personal potential.

Responsibility – We Must Own It

Before we move on, let's go back to the first step – owning. If you stop and think about any kind of responsibility, you must take ownership. When we are striving to take necessary actions, it is our responsibility to own them. Like trust within ourselves, being responsible for our actions is a choice. As in all values, responsibility comes from within. Taking responsibility in living happily and effectively, is a choice we all make or don't. For instance, if we perceive life as external, we have no control and subject ourselves to be a victim of any number of circumstances that come our way. This is where responsibility comes into action. The ability to think in a positive manner, respond with focus, and take charge of our life lies within us. Life is about taking responsibility for it.

We have no control over most events, but we do have control over how we respond to them. In other words, some things in life are just beyond our control. Conversely, many things are within it. It is how we respond to these things that makes the difference. An important part of responding is accepting responsibility for the results that we have direct control of.

Again, as we have discussed previously, one of our biggest barriers to responsibility is admitting when we make a mistake. First, we must own up to our mistakes. Then secondly, admitting when we're wrong about something. When these occur, we are taking full responsibility for ownership. Taking full responsibility is also understanding we make no excuses, nor do we blame anyone else when things go wrong. So, if things don't go well, accept responsibility for the situation and take action to correct, change, or improve it.

Our life is not perfect. No one person is perfect. When you have the courage and character to admit to your mistakes and take responsibility, those around you will appreciate the honesty and respect you more for it.

So, we talked about combating our barriers through some principles of 'act as if' and positive self-talk, making the right choices, then developing trust, confidence, taking appropriate risks, and finally, responsibility. To stay focused upon our efforts, we must have a process in place. This process will act as key skills for success regarding combating our barriers. Here is a ten-part process that can be applied to keep us focused upon combating and confronting any barriers that exist that may detain us from taking the necessary actions to learn and grow:

1. Your vision. Imagine that there are no limitations, no fears, no assumptions, there are, in essence, no barriers on what actions you could take. Now imagine completing these actions with trust within yourself and the abilities to see these actions through.

2. Your values. What are your most important values in life, and what order of importance do they exist for you? In combating barriers to act, taking responsibility is one of the most important values to have. The greater clarity you have regarding your values, the easier it will be to taking necessary actions, as your values are linked to your actions.

3. Your mission. This is where your trust within and self-confidence comes in. The mission will guide you to bringing about positive change regarding removing barriers as so to take the committed actions you need to complete to learn and grow from.

4. Your purpose. This is the reason you get out of bed in the morning. The reason you do what you're currently doing rather than worrying about any self-imposed barriers regarding any fears, assumptions, or possibility of failure.

5. Your choices. We must choose to act. Not always easy but taking the necessary actions after we reflect upon an experience will result in learning and growing opportunities.

6. Your risks. Effectively implementing your vision, values, mission, and purpose will; at times, involve taking risks. If you trust yourself within and are willing to take full responsibility for your life, you will then take appropriate risks according to the actions that are required. (I am sure at this point you're beginning to see how each component of this process works together with the other to be successful.)

7. Your action goals. These are the specific, written, measurable, time-bounded goals that you want to achieve sometime in the future, based upon your values, vision, mission, and purpose. Taking necessary actions according to reflective experiences that need results should be taken seriously.

8. Your priorities. These are the most important actions you want to complete. Your ability to set priorities, to determine the most valuable use of your time relative to achieving your action goals, is the key to removing your barriers.

9. Your demonstrated actions. These are the committed actions you take to achieve results from your reflective experiences. Determine the specific actions that you need to take immediately to extinguish the most daunting barriers standing in your way of taking the actions you must accomplish.

10. Lastly, follow-up. Did your actions result in success or failure? You can't answer this question unless you follow through the entire process. And remember, even if failure is the answer, it will also be your greatest teacher. All reflective experiences begin and end with your thoughts. This last step in the process is critical to your overall results.

Using this ten-part process will help you identify any barriers, resolve them, as so you can then focus upon the actions you must take when reflecting upon that undeniable compelling urge to act that comes with life's experiences that long for your attention.

Most barriers are those we allow. Once we allow the barriers to enter, we also accept them. Much of life is worrying about 'what if'. It's a barrier of not knowing what our future holds. But if we stop worrying about the 'what ifs' and we start worrying about the 'what is', we now have the power to engage with our most urgent challenges – in the present – and actually do something about them today.

One common obstacle is limitations regarding our learning opportunities. It is when we limit our abilities that learning is not possible. What we must do is to choose differently. We all have a choice as to our own limitations. Don't limit yourself when you know deep within you can do more. Learning will have a few obstacles just as there are obstacles to our growth. How will you choose?

CHAPTER 5

CALL TO ACTION – THOUGHTS & EMOTIONS

OUR INNER DRIVE

Inner Drive. You say, drive? Yes. Drive indicates activeness. This drive, as I refer to, is more than an intent to do something, it's a confirmation to do it. Yet another way to think of drive is on the dashboard of your car. Put your car into 'drive' and it moves forward. The more pressure on your acceleration pedal, the faster you move forward. This same idea is how our inner drive works. Moving forward and the more effort you put into this 'drive' the further you go in life.

Our inner drive is not passive, but considerably stronger than mere interest. This drive is initiated with passion to create the compelling actions motivated by our reflective experiences. Our efforts that take us beyond reflecting begin with our inner drive. No matter how active we are, how much effort we make, our state of consciousness creates our world, and if there is no change on that inner level, no amount of action will make any difference. So, we begin with a focus of our inner drive regarding thoughts and emotions.

Not what you do, but how you do what you do determines whether you are fulfilling your destiny. And how you do what you do is determined by your inner drive. Once our inner drive is examined and prepared to move to the next step, our outer drive, we can now take the committed actions to promote learning, then personal growth that will guide us to our personal potential.

Let's go back to the word – committed. Why is this important regarding our actions? It is when we commit ourselves to doing something, that we make a special pact to physically doing it.

All effective actions are the results of compelling evidence that dictate such acts. It is this compelling evidence that creates the motivation to act. This inner drive of motivation is what I refer to as your call to action.

Why is this 'call' so important? Because it's in the answering of this call that demonstrative actions are acquired. Where do these calls come from? These calls are speaking to you from within as you reflect upon your life's experiences. What are these calls speaking of? They are telling us that there is importance regarding our reflective experiences and that there are actions required of us. So important, that it is in the completion of these actions that learning and personal growing is possible.

Demonstrating effective actions are the foundational keys to success. It is in this success that results in personal growth is accomplished. But, before action, there is an internal process. In other words, there is a process that involves an inner drive that completes the cycle of thoughts and emotions.

Let's pause right here. Inner drive. We touched on this term in the beginning of this, and the first chapter as well. It is this inner drive that indicates activeness and assertiveness. Again, this drive, as I refer to, is more than an intent to do something, it's a confirmation to do it. Not what you do, but how you do what you do determines whether you are fulfilling your destiny. And how you do what you do is determined by your inner drive. Yes. The 'how' is designed by and a confirmation of our thoughts and feelings, or our inner drive. The 'how' is the confirmation, energy, and motivation to move into actions. So, once our inner drive is examined and prepared, we can move to the next step, our outer drive. Beginning with the inner drive, your journey then continues with an outer drive, or demonstrative physical actions you take, but it all begins within.

Further, it is your outer drive that arrives at your goal through the physical actions taken only after the inner, reflective experience has occurred. These actions match what you want to accomplish, what you desire, and the results of what you want according to these actions. We will discuss more regarding our outer drive; or the act of answering the call, in a later chapter.

Inner drive is regarding the present – right now. So, are actions always taken promptly? Not always, but your inner drive is continually working in the present while you are in reflection. As for demonstrative actions, there are times that our proposed actions require additional time to develop a plan of action. These plans for action could be responding with more thoughts, emotional positions that need time to actualize, or even a detailed plan. These things occur within. This could be thought as the planning stage for the outer drive.

Intentionally Present

As we know, we cannot change the past, nor can we do anything about the future. The actions you take today are all about the present. Why now, why the present? Because where we reside is in the present. In other words, living in the present moment while giving thought to the actions necessary, will motivate you to move forward with those actions. That is what the inner drive is all about. Again, this drive provides us the motivation to take the next step in actually answering the call to act with demonstrative actions to learn and grow from our reflective experiences.

The present is another way to think – 'what is' – can only be described as where you live today. So, make a positive impact right now, for it is the present that you can change today. The only way to change today is to complete the actions that you are compelled to complete from your reflective experiences. And if change is needed immediately, the actions must also be immediate. Why wait to only delay actions that can improve your life? Walk away from yesterday, don't think about tomorrow, take the appropriate actions, then learn and grow from them – now.

Let's go into more detail regarding the present. An inner drive regarding a call to action requires us to be in the moment, focused, and intentionally present. Let's leave it right there for a moment – intentionally. It is our intentions that guide our actions. So, if we are not intentionally present during our inner drive process, we may miss some essential information vital for taking actions. What's the consequences if we're not present? The consequences could be anything from missing out on the intended learning from the reflective experience to that of overlooking the experience altogether. Too busy? Not important? Whatever the self-imposed excuse, learning and growing is sacrificed.

Being efficient and intentionally present is a function of our inner drive. With this kind of focus, the most effective plans of action can take place. Demonstrated actions happen in the present, so you must be internally present. Being present is not difficult; it's just to simply pause and reflect. Being present, or your complete thought process of being self-aware of all things that come before you, is a vital part regarding your actions that you take after you reflect upon an experience. Let me stress here that it takes an intentional effort to be completely present with oneself. This type of inner concentration of thought is requiring us to use all our senses and focus upon all of life's experiences.

With that said, awareness is the key to all our senses. We must always be keenly aware of our surroundings. Without pausing for all things in life, you will most likely miss some of the important things around you, events that happen to you, and more importantly, in you.

Remember that a call to action is based upon your inner drive. This call to action is the foundation to the physical actions you will demonstrate on the outside, or your outer drive. It's important to understand that we cannot move to our outer drive without first fully experiencing our inner drive process. This is an intentional, thought-provoking focus, one that allows us to be completely self-aware of first, planning our actions, then second, implementing those actions. Remember that the self-awareness and planning stages for necessary actions are the functions of our inner drive.

Being present isn't always easy, but if you're completely focused, you will not miss any of life's experiences. An easy way to remember pausing for any experience is the focus of what truly matters, and that is what's happening within you right now.

Being completely mindful is living in the moment. It requires that an inner part of you pauses from the external part to step back and simply experience each event as it unfolds. It takes deep concentration of thought to truly notice what you are experiencing. It's what I refer to as *experiencing the experience*. To experience the experience fully, significance and actions are essential. This significance indicates that if any event truly matters to you, you will take the necessary time to experience it fully with inner purposeful thoughts and emotions.

Prepare, Release, and Reflect

So, let's discuss more regarding what steps are necessary during this process of inner drive. There are three important steps that include: preparing our inner drive thoughts, releasing our emotions, and the value of reflection before action. So, in addition to being intentionally present, we must continue our inner focus by preparing our minds, releasing our feelings, then go further into reflection in making decisions regarding the actions we will take from our experiences. These steps are a part of our inner drive process and the call to action. It is these steps that must be intentional in thoughts, feelings, and responses. Further, these vital steps will inspire you to reach deep within, to truly reflect upon your past and present experiences. By going deep within, you can connect to reflective experiences with not just any response, but life-changing intentional actions that can promote effective learning, then growing.

Let's go into more detail regarding each step of the process of preparing, releasing, and reflecting:

Step One - Preparing Our Inner Drive

In preparing, our inner drive allows us to shape our thoughts, inspire and stretch our feelings, and then apply the understanding of our life's lessons as a result of the actions we fulfill.

The first thing you must do in preparing is to find a quiet place to sit and close your eyes to be completely centered. Your location should have minimal distractions. Preparing requires relaxation, which also means no movement. Once you have a quiet place, focus on your breath. Take several slow inhalations, exhaling slowly and completely. Lastly, pause deeply for the reflections to enter your soul. When we take our thoughts and emotion to this level, there may be a mixture of both joy and sadness.

Why this mixture of joy and sadness? Let's go into more detail. It's only a fact of life that we all experience positive and negative events. Everyone loves when something positive happens in their life, but having a negative situation occur is not the end of the world. Why? Because we can find positive benefits even in the worst of times. One great benefit is the lessons we learn. It is usually from these negative experiences that we encounter valuable life lessons and have opportunities for deeper understanding of our self-awareness which effects personal growth.

Step Two - Releasing Our Emotions
Now open your eyes, as well as your mind, and especially your inner drive emotions. It's like this – with your mind, thoughts are presented and through your feelings, emotions are released. These emotions are filled with natural energy that helps us as we make decisions to act upon our reflective experiences. It is the combination of these thoughts and emotions that produce the responses that lead to proposed actions from our reflections.

This is also an opportune time to ask yourself questions but first, simply respond to the reflection, then, determine what actions you could take regarding the reflection. I believe one of the first questions we should be asking ourselves is 'why'. For example: Why do we think it's important to act upon our reflective experiences? Answering this question of 'why' then provides motivation to initiate our inner drive and 'why' it is so important to the success of the next phase of acting upon our reflective experiences.

The most important answers lead us to taking appropriate actions, which then results in learning and growing from the experiences. Once we find our 'why' internally, we then prompt our outer drive for actions. But first, we must fulfill the internal drive reflective process.

Step Three - The Value of Reflection Before Actions

As we discussed in Chapter 1, reflection is a vital part of the process of connecting to our experiences, more importantly are the actions, in responding to these experiences. Reflecting is the foundation to the inner drive. In reflecting, many people do not recognize the value that once they have reflected upon thoughts and emotions regarding their experiences, that they just let them go without doing anything about them. In other words, through reflecting upon experiences you had, and even recognizing there is a good lesson from them yet doing nothing with them – no follow through with demonstrated actions to grow from the experiences. The true value of intentional reflections is to take actions after you have deeply thought about the potential learning that come from present and past experiences. And with learning comes growing.

When intentionally reflecting, you must understand that every thought and emotion has the potential to go to the next level of demonstrated action and be applied in a way that growth can be maximized. How exciting and motivating is this? As exciting and motivating this may sound, we still need to act upon them.

Now that we have discovered the importance of preparing our inner drive thoughts, releasing our emotions, and understanding the value of reflection before actions, there are more things to consider regarding this call to action ...

Considering Your Viewpoints Before Action

Before we submit to the physical nature of taking necessary actions regarding our reflective experiences, we need to consider how we view each experience. A viewpoint begins with a thought but is released with emotions. These emotions are released with a positive or negative attitude attached depending how we view the experiences we are reflecting upon. This is the emotional energy before the actions are taken. This process then provides the motivation for our inner drive to initiate the plan of proposed actions. All points of views while in reflection will make a significant difference regarding the level of success of the action that is taken after each reflection you experience.

Positive and Negative Viewpoints

Life is a series of outcomes – both positive and negative. For many of us, we want more of the positive experiences and would like to just forget about the negative occurrences. The positive outcomes we try to repeat, but it is from the negative experiences that we learn and grow the greatest. This learning is known as the 'hard knocks' of life. It is these 'hard knocks' that teaches us in a powerful and impactful way. From the results, we can make positive choices to learn by them, or negatively defeat ourselves.

If you want to achieve more in life, you must learn to move forward no matter the outcome. Unfortunately, so many of us look at negative outcomes as failures. These outcomes I speak of, are those actions we took from our reflective experiences.

Think in these terms: We reflected upon an experience, we thought about what we want to do regarding the experience, and we took what we thought to be appropriate action. The next step in the reflective process is now to review the results of this action. What if the results end in failure? Failure sounds and feels negative. If we want to positively change our lives, we must turn this negative feeling into a positive. First, understand that failing does not make failures of us – it is the attitude in which we respond to each outcome that truly defines us.

It truly matters whether there is a viewpoint of negative or positive while reflecting. A negative viewpoint will result in negative outcomes regarding the actions you take. Being negative while reflecting will only bring stress and despair. But remember, it is a choice as to the viewpoint you choose. Yet the best point of view to choose is being positive. To be more positive, all you must do is think differently. It's not always easy but thinking differently will create new perspectives. These new perspectives will result in more positive actions and outcomes. Not all outcomes will be as positive as we would like them to be but even in the worst of circumstances, we can always find something positive from those actions and a possible learning opportunity.

It will be important for you to refocus upon a positive point of view while in reflection concerning an experience. Remember that your viewpoint begins with what you think, and it is your thoughts that are the foundation of each reflective experience. After inner drive thoughts, then staying emotionally positive and your actions will be positive as well. With positive results, growth is possible. In growth, we move closer to our personal potential.

Staying Positive Before Taking Proposed Actions

We know the best viewpoint before we take actions is to be positive. Let's take it a step further. Our viewpoint is the foundation to our attitude. The call to action requires us to focus on our emotional strengths within while reflecting upon our experiences. A good place to start is our attitude. Our attitude is a quality. This quality is shown on the outside. It defines us. I like to think that our viewpoint begins with our inner drive and is shown as an attitude through our actions.

The most effective attitude is to be positive while reflecting. Staying positive is not always easy but being positive while taking actions will provide the best learning environment. Why? Because, as already mentioned, our actions are not always on-point, we make mistakes along the way. Remember, it is by our mistakes that we learn the most. Staying positive is an extra effort especially when we believe we have made a mistake. The key to staying positive is first thinking positive. When we reflect, the viewpoint in which we choose will determine the outcome of the experience we have.

Maintaining a positive attitude regardless of any past negative events can be difficult, but if we focus upon our attitude and think positive while in reflection, we have a better chance of staying that way. It is when we start and finish with a positive attitude while reflecting that we experience the most effective actions seized.

Okay, let's go back to the idea of staying positive. So, it's not always easy to stay positive. Well, it's not. Negativity is all around us – in the newspaper, on the television, on our social media – everywhere. What if your reflective experience is a difficult, negative event? That's why it's not always easy. There are times we allow the external world to affect us internally. My question is – why do we allow it? It is when we allow the negative, that we also accept the negative.

This is not to say that negative things don't happen, because they do, and they are a part of life, but you can choose how you respond to negative experiences with a positive attitude. Wait a minute – this is crazy! You're telling me that if something negative has occurred in our life, to look for something positive in it? Yes! If you truly reflect upon the experience, I believe you will always find at least one thing positive in it – but, you must look for it.

The problem exists when we allow these misfortunes and circumstances to weigh us down. It is during these challenging times that we have a choice as to how we want to respond while reflecting upon them. If our attitude regarding the experience is negative, these damaging thoughts and feelings will have an undesirable toll on us physically, mentally, and spiritually. If we allow these misfortunes to affect us, they will bring us down and make it difficult to rise back up within especially while in reflection.

Choosing Positive

Okay. We discussed staying positive before taking proposed actions, then if we can sustain this positive attitude, we are now also choosing it. Choosing to be positive is evidence that your inner drive is taking charge. (We will discuss more regarding choices as they relate to our growth in a later chapter.) My own experiences have been based on possessing, and in most instances, demonstrating a positive point of view – by choice. No one forces another have a negative point of view – it is by personal choice. I learned long ago to be grateful while in reflection for what I have and make the choice to be positive and happy.

Living a positive, upbeat life is something most of us want; but like most things in life – being positive is a choice you alone make. You must choose to be positive and focus on staying that way throughout your actions. It is an emotion that starts with your inner drive while reflecting and is demonstrated on the outside by your actions.

So, we have now discussed 'how to' organize our inner drive through our choices of viewpoints and remaining positive. Let's go into detail regarding the emotional qualities needed to create effective actions.

A Choice of Assertiveness for Taking Actions

Yet another inner drive quality is assertiveness. Just as positive or negative attitudes are choices, so is being assertive. Being assertive begins with our inner drive and is a behavior we demonstrate through our words and more importantly, our actions. Creating a positive and assertive nature will serve you well for effective reflection and successful outcomes.

66

What about being assertive? Well, if we begin reflecting upon any experience with passive thoughts, our feelings and responses will be passive as well. That's not going to be effective while taking the necessary actions after your inner drive process is complete. Why not be assertive? As we begin our reflections, it's always best to start with assertive thoughts. These assertive thoughts are at the peak of our inner drive process. Being assertive is an emotional quality that determines our point of view. When we think about being assertive, it is a quality that is more focused on positive actions. Then the opposite is true when we are aggressive. Think about it in these terms: passive, assertive, or aggressive. We know that nothing comes from being passive. What about being aggressive? It is when we choose aggressiveness that our reflections turn to more negative outcomes. So, the best choice is being assertive. Think about it this way: If we begin our reflection with an assertive mindset, then the call to action process will match with proposed assertive actions.

To be assertive is also taking charge of our future regarding where and what we want to be in life. To have this directed point of view in our mind, provides a sense of freedom. We choose what kind of life we want. One that can promote a motivating and exhilarating feeling. The more assertive we are, the more reflective experiences we can strive for. This positive power is the energy within our inner drive while reflecting that generates the assertive emotions. It is with these assertive emotions that we risk moving forward to take appropriate actions regardless of the possible barriers in front of us.

Are There Barriers to Being Assertive?

As we discovered in the previous chapter, barriers can stop us from acting, but only if we allow them to. Are you afraid that if you assert yourself and move towards the things you desire; they will not work out? So, you never take risks? What if you were to think and reflect differently? Assertiveness is only effective if used. You begin with thinking and reflecting with an assertive point of view as you begin taking positive actions according to your experiences.

In response to most reflective experiences, good things just do not happen to us – it is the extra effort and passion put forth in taking the committed actions to get what we want in life. Passion is the assertiveness behind the energy of any action taken. It's assertiveness that we focus on during our reflections that create the results we are striving for. This passionate effort is the willpower that keeps us moving forward while reflecting regardless of any barriers put in front of our progress. The actions of taking this type of initiative is from our level of intensity regarding assertiveness within us for the duration of our reflection experience. The most rewarding things are the results of our own individual assertive efforts regarding our actions and the attainment of achieving what we want most in life.

During reflection, if we have the right emotional attitude about it, we will never exhaust our capacity to move toward our personal potential. Notice the key word is 'move' – assertiveness is a positive viewpoint that is always in a forward motion while taking actions.

It is true that we all possess the capability and strong desire in our thoughts and emotions to accomplish what we want. It is usually buried deep within. This desire is a thunderous inner voice of our reflective thoughts and feelings – we all possess assertiveness – we only need to let go of anything holding us back from moving forward with positive, assertive actions. It is through our powerful inner drive that reflection experiences offer positive thoughts when initiated. With reflective thoughts such as this, anything is possible.

Patience to Act

Yet another call to act is the quality of being patient before taking the required actions from our reflective experiences. (We talked about patience during reflection in the first chapter.) So, if there is an emotional inner drive quality that should be focused upon before acting more often, it should be patience. Before the attitude arrives while in reflection, there is the point of view you must consider. This gap in arrival time is patience. When we are not patient; especially while reflecting and connecting, we can miss important opportunities of experiencing the actions, lessons, and applied learning of the intended reflective experience altogether.

One important discipline that can be enhanced for many of us is our patience. Patience is a vital component of effective actions. Why? Because there will be some reflections that take time to develop. It will be patience throughout our reflections that will determine the results of our actions.

A great example would be while reflecting upon our fast-paced world, we witness many people that seem to be always in a hurry to go here and there to achieve things in life. Are these same people always effective in achieving the actions they set out to do? The answer is – no. Being in a hurry, we tend to miss important steps along the way. Again, it is by being patient while in reflection, that we are thoughtful throughout each step we must take to achieve the most effective action we want from our reflective experiences.

An attitude of patience while reflecting is not just an important inner drive quality, it's a virtue. For example, hard work is when we exert extra effort to gain results. Note that the hard work comes first, then the results. Those with little patience while reflecting, want the outcome, or result before the time and effort required to receive it. The confidence in knowing our hard work will lead to well-deserved success

69

is through patience. As they say – *good things in life are worth the wait.*

Waiting with the right attitude equals patience while in reflection. Patience, like many disciplines, comes from within your inner drive, which also means that you manage it. With patience, good things happen for and to you – at the right date, time, and place. Embrace patience while proposing committed actions and receive long-lasting positive results.

Faith While Acting

Another emotional quality that comes from our inner drive is faith. When faith is entered into the call to action, it creates an inner strength that helps us along the way. Because faith is based upon the unseen and unknown, it many times is associated with things that haven't occurred as yet. Case in point here is that when we reflect upon the future, we must put faith in ourselves that we will take the most effective and appropriate actions when required.

There are two points of view regarding the future. One is in faith; the other is fear. There is a significant difference between the two emotions. Fear believes in a negative future and faith believes in a positive future. As previously mentioned in the last chapter, our fears must be faced while in reflection. It is faith within ourselves that helps us face our fears. When using faith while reflecting, it will not only help us to face our fears, but to overcome them as well.

While in reflection, faith has no boundaries – it is only when we put barriers in our thoughts and emotions that our faith is in question. Faith is something we must reflect upon and believe in. Faith can represent many things to many people. It is encouraging when it seems there is nothing else to depend on, we can reflect upon our faith within to help us get through the most difficult of times in life. It is this idea of *getting through,* that our encouraging, demonstrative actions play an important role regarding our results. It's true, faith focuses upon encouragement. Everyone loves encouragement – it lifts us up when we are down and motivates us when we are discouraged. When we put faith in ourselves as we reflect, we are providing much needed encouragement.

Too many of us lose faith during the challenging times in our lives. Unfortunately, many do this because they are afraid of failure. The reality is that these difficulties seldom defeat us – it is the lack of faith, especially while reflecting, that usually does.

Responding with authority after reflecting upon an experience is having the quality of faith in our abilities to take necessary action when required. With this kind of power, anything is possible. This faith within provides us with confidence in our ability to move forward with actions regardless of the obstacles. Having this quality while reflecting will most often bring success to our actions.

Whether it be never giving in or never giving up – the quality of faith is sometimes all we have or truly need as we reflect upon our life. Even in the most difficult of times, faith is what we should hold on to most – it is sometimes the only difference between quitting and moving forward with required calls to action in life.

A call to action is an inner drive of thoughts and emotions that are the focus within while reflecting upon our experiences in life. To accomplish this, in this chapter, we must understand to begin our call to act, we need to be completely self-aware and intentionally present in our thought process. We also must weigh out our positive and negative viewpoints before acting. Further, that to experience success regarding our actions, we must choose to be positive.

Once we have our positive attitude set, we then move to our emotional inner drive qualities to embrace assertiveness, patience, and having faith and believing in ourselves. We are now ready to take the next steps in the process.

We must now get our heart right. In this chapter we discussed how important our inner drive of thinking and emotions were vital for taking appropriate actions. In our next chapter, we go beyond mere thoughts and emotions to responses of our inner drive of the heart ...

CHAPTER 6

CALL TO ACTION – DESIRE, PURPOSE, & PATH

INNER DRIVE OF THE HEART

In the previous chapter we discussed our call to action using our inner drive of thoughts and feelings. We now go beyond mere thoughts and feelings to the inner drive of the heart. In fact, the most powerful inner drive function is our heart. It is our heart that will provide the necessary desire and purpose that will be put into our firm actions we take according to our reflective experiences.

So, why go beyond our thoughts and feelings? It is because our heart encompasses all emotions in one. In this one place, when all emotions are used together, they provide us the strongest emotional guide regarding our response from our thoughts and feelings. And it is through this expressive guide from our heart that takes us closer to appropriate actions.

In this chapter, we will touch upon many emotions of the heart. Some like: being focused, discipline, motivation, encouragement, and love. With these strong emotions of the heart, they represent how our emotions can follow a path to proposed actions for results from our reflective experiences. But before we get into these emotions that lead us to actions, we must decide what we want and why we want it. In other words, what do we desire and for what purpose.

Let's pause for a moment. Desire and purpose. They are indeed from the heart. What roles do they play as we contemplate what actions we will take? Let's break them down. First, there is desire, or *what* you want, followed by purpose, or the *why* you want it. What's missing? What's missing is the last step before moving forward to act. It's *how*, or the path that we must follow to get it.

Now, for a moment, go back to our inner drive functions of thoughts and feelings. It is once we have reflected upon these thoughts and feelings, that the process then takes us to making decisions based upon our proposed actions. Note that I state both thoughts and feelings. Based upon our thoughts, our feelings about those thoughts are then released. When you add the emotional element of feelings, it brings your heart into a dimension of bonding with the experience and makes it more personal to you. And when things are personal to us, we are motivated to act upon them. Again, it provides us with the desire, or what we want, followed by the purpose of why we want it. When an experience is experienced in this way, it is closing the full cycle of thought, feeling, and response. But this is no ordinary response. This response is going beyond our thoughts and feelings. This inner drive emotional response of desire and purpose is your heart speaking to you.

Meaning and Purpose

I think it's important to first share my perspective on this topic. I see meaning and purpose as slightly different entities. Many times, we see them together as one focus. I believe there are two distinct differences between meaning and purpose. To me, meaning provides the energy to focus upon your purpose. It is the meaning regarding your purpose that gives us the reasons to do what we do. The true meaning in life answers the question of why we are here doing what we were meant to do. Reflecting upon your own individual meaning in life consists of a deep concentration of asking yourself a long and diverse list of questions regarding your purpose. Questions like: 'What do I see myself genuinely enjoying time after time and can't seem to get enough of?' and 'What gives me a reason to look forward to each day?' then 'What do I do and get lost in time without really noticing?' When you can answer these questions, you will also find your purpose.

Meaning and purpose go together. You need first, meaning as the foundation to help produce your purpose. Identifying and embracing meaning and purpose while in reflection then provides you with direction regarding how you will make a difference in your life. This meaning and purpose leads to learning. It is the passion behind your purpose that wants you to learn. The more learning, the more growing.

If you have not reflected upon your personal meaning and purpose in life, it is time you did. Why? Because there is nothing more energizing than to realize the power of meaning and your purpose in life. When we find this true meaning, we are energized and passionate about life. Being energized, we produce inner drive thoughts about our meaning and purpose with enthusiastic feelings that want to be continually released through our positive outer drive actions. These powerful inner drive functions then create so much excitement that we want to learn, we want to grow. So much so, that when we experience this learning and growing, we in turn create an overwhelming feeling of success. Success in knowing that we are living our purpose!

Unfortunately, some people wander through life and never quite find their own individual meaning. Remember, this meaning is the motivation that is the foundation to your purpose. Is it that we don't want to do the necessary work to find meaning? Are we fearful that things won't work out regarding our purpose? Whatever the reason, without meaning, there can be no compelling purpose. Meaning answers your calling, or purpose in life. It is the combination of your meaning and purpose that creates fulfillment in your life. The key to a fulfilled life is finding it – we must look for it by starting within our inner drive of the heart. What does our heart tell us? What gives us energy and excitement throughout the day? Reflecting and answering these questions will help us find our meaning, that in turn, will lead us to our purpose in life.

What is the motivation behind meaning? Simply, it is the ability to be grounded in your life's purpose. Being grounded in life is living your life understanding and demonstrating your purpose each day. When we take the extra efforts to demonstrate our purpose, we are indeed going beyond our reflective experiences to create actions behind the purpose.

This grounding also provides understanding while reflecting to how and why we live life. We all look for meaning to find our purpose. Some of us have found it, others of us are still searching. It is different for each one of us, but you must find meaning for your purpose.

As for meaning, it creates the energy for our purpose to flourish, it takes a tremendous amount of deep inner drive thought, reflection, providing extra effort, and time to find your true purpose in life. Like I have mentioned, there are those that quit and give up finding their purpose because they do not want to take the necessary time and effort in searching for it. This search is supplied only by our meaning. Without meaning, you will fall short in finding your purpose in life. I personally cannot imagine a life without meaning, lacking purpose.

Possessing meaning in life requires the willingness to push the limits and break the barriers to reach the pinnacle in which meaning is an inner-most part of us. To find true meaning calls for us to go deep within our inner drive and become more reflective toward what we genuinely care about most in life. This type of meaningful focus and reflection includes giving ourselves the time and space to think independently, and to value the inward journey and connection that leads us in pursuing the true meaning of our purpose.

Being Focused

One key factor of this chapter is to be focused as we are being called to act. In other words, having focused reflections of inner drive emotions of the heart, we can then take actions to the intended learning of each reflection that occurs. This will promote personal growth which is the goal of all reflective experiences that will lead us to our personal potential.

Another way to consider these focused efforts is a deep self-awareness of *thinking about what you want to think about*. With this self-awareness, you get to choose what you want to reflect upon, thus taking the appropriate actions needed. It's because you are going beyond just thinking and feeling regarding your experiences, to being emotionally connected and responding with the question: 'What must I do?' This then is followed by: 'Why must I do it?' Remember, it is our desire of the heart that decides the *what* answer. It is then the purpose, or *why* that follows providing the reasons for the proposed actions needed.

The first question referring to what you must do is usually easier to answer. The hardest to figure out is the *why* you must do it. I will also tell you that we must discover our *what* before the *why* arrives.

It is with focused and actionable responses you take after your reflections that the proposed learning begins to take shape. It's truly going beyond your thoughts and feelings and exerting efforts of engaging the necessary emotional responses of your inner drive of the heart that create the foundation of learning based upon your reflective experiences.

What Do You Really Want?

As I have already mentioned, the *what* we want comes relativity easy, but the *why* we want it is the area of real effort. Before taking any actions regarding your reflective experiences, you must know what you want from them. What we want comes from our inner desire of the heart. In the case of pursuing personal potential: Is it enhanced learning? Personal growth? In other words, what's the goal?

The answer will provide the clue as to what you really desire or want. You are only committed to the choices you make. Start creating what you want in your mind, then have a reflective experience that initiates your inner drive to act. Feel that way, be that way, and imagine it happening the way you want it to happen.

Our Heart's Desire

Desires of the heart become very emotional as we focus upon what we want to do with these desires. What we want and where we want to go in life are the things we desire most. It is these reflective experiences that provide direction and purpose for our desires.

Daily reflection will lead us to wonderful things, but we must first have desire during reflection to help us move from where we are today, to where we want to go tomorrow. It's all about what we want. Desire is a strong emotional feeling that can seem overpowering at times. And where do you think this desire comes from? You guessed it – your inner drive of the heart! This is not just any kind of desire, but one of passionate desire – the power to move forward in any overwhelming circumstance that comes before us to passionately launch ourselves into something we want in life. And what we want in life will require a call for committed actions.

Even while reflecting upon life, our desires keep us motivated to strive for all things we want. It is a strong desire alone that can keep us motivated and move us forward when there seems to be nothing else; mentally or physically, that we can give. And when we add *why* we want it; we now have good reason to move to *how*, or the path we will choose to get it.

As desire comes from the heart, our reflections go deep within. Desire is another deep emotion of the heart. It is where our most essential values and roadmap to actions are kept and held. It is only with desire to focus on what we want that the heart also listens. As in any reflective experience, if we listen deeply to our heart, it will in turn listen to us and help lead us to the committed actions we will need to take for growth.

Responding with ability is to allow desire to live within the inner drive of the heart. With passion and desire, nothing can stand in the way from taking the necessary actions regarding what you want in life. As we initiate the strength we have in this emotion of desire, it will enable us to achieve anything, even the seemingly impossible if we remain focused throughout reflective experiences, and then followed with appropriate and committed actions.

Your Purpose for Taking Actions
For actions to be successful, we must have a purpose to do them. Look at it this way – why go to the trouble to act upon something without having a purpose to do it? Well, the answer is that this purpose acts as the *why* you are taking the actions you know you

need to take. Our purpose answers the questions regarding *why* we want to take committed actions to attain something. For the 'purposes' of this book, we want to take the appropriate actions according to the reflective experiences that occur throughout our lives. The purpose acts as the energy within the reflection to move us from beyond our thoughts and feelings, to strong emotional responses of the heart, then to outer drive actions that will lead us to our personal potential.

More On 'Why'

Reflections upon our life will usually come with questions attached. The effect of these questions also creates a feeling of tension that these same questions must be addressed. Many questions start with – *why*. Let's go into more detail that answers the question – Why must I do it?

'Why did we do this' and *'why we didn't do that'* are often the leading questions we ask ourselves while in reflection. It is when we ask ourselves *why* during our reflective experiences that the opportunity for learning more about ourselves is at its best. It is true that when we engage ourselves into reflective experiences, we often ask ourselves questions. When it comes to *why* certain things happen – or do not happen – to us; the reasons can be elusive.

One of the biggest issues that affect us all is *why* we didn't do something when all our thoughts and feelings were directing us to take some kind of action. We all want to know the answers of *why* we didn't take the appropriate actions when we needed to. The answers will vary, but sometimes things just happen or don't occur at all with no explanation. When we reflect, if we combine the inner drive of our heart, we can then better understand the reasons *why* these things happened or not.

We have all struggled with the – *why* – certain things happen to and in our lives. Is it fate? Is it meant to be? There are many that believe everything happens for a reason. This belief then often leads to possible answers of identifying a possible cause, or why a life altering event occurred that you experienced. This going back to the idea that everything happens for a reason and at the right time in your life.

The response is – yes – things do and will continue to happen to us and within us, with no explanation at all. The key is to expect these things – positive and negative – to be a part of our journey in life. As these events, situations, or even people that enter in and out of our lives, they will impress memories when they leave us. Deep reflection will help us find the *why* answers to the questions during and after these unique life experiences.

If we reflect upon following our inner drive with the passionate emotions within our heart, it can lead us to the answers we seek. It will be by deep reflection, that many answers can be found. It is also important that during reflection that if we lead with our heart – positive things will happen most often.

When we ask ourselves questions, there is a feeling of pulling and pushing to find the answers. This natural pull and push is the passion we talked about earlier. These answers also provide us with meaning and reasons as to *why* these events or situations happen to us. If we have a clear picture of our inner drive of what has meaning to us and express it by using our heart as a guide, we can indeed find the reasons *why*. In other words, the meaning then happens within us.

Your *why* answers the question regarding what inner drive path you decide to follow. Yes. Once our *why* has been answered, we move to the next step in the process. Now, we move to *how*, or the path we will take that includes our proposed actions. But when it truly comes down to which path to follow, it is then our inner drive of the heart that guides us. Does this make sense? Look at it this way – when you follow your heart, you are taking the path that your inner drive has chosen. As this relates to a call for actions, no one accomplishes effective actions without a purposeful path to follow. It is this same path that leads us to learning and growth.

So, stop there for a moment. If indeed this path leads us to learning and growth, it also acts as a foundation to the *how* that proceeds the appropriate actions. Further, it is both learning and growth that will provide us with continued motivation to follow this path. Why is this? It is because of this purposeful path that provides us a clearer picture or the foundation of the *how* this path will lead us to the proposed actions we will take.

It is not until you ask and answer the question of *why*, that your direction of *what actions* to take is then clearly identified. So, it is *what* we want to accomplish, *why* we want it, and *how* we will proceed in getting it. These are all inner drive functions that must be completed before outer drive actions begin. Are you following this process? Not always easy, but truly reflect upon this process. It will make sense.

There is much reflection time spent during this important planning phase and when you get your answers you are looking for; you will then put all your motivational emotions of passion and enthusiasm into your direction. With your inner drive providing the answers, you will be tremendously motivated and confident to strive toward proposed outer drive actions.

If we are to strive toward a proposal for committed actions, there must be a process in place. This process is comprised of steps that will assist you in planning and implementing necessary actions regarding your reflective experiences. These initial steps come from within, then move forward to the outside through the actions we take. The biggest mistakes come from trying to take actions before completely preparing our inner drive steps first.

Here is a four-step process to lead us from our heart's desires of 'what' we want and 'why', or our reasons for wanting it. Then lastly, we address the 'how' we are going to get what we want. The 'how' is the last step in the inner drive process and is the path we take to the proposed actions to learn and grow from our reflective experiences.

Step 1 - Affirm Actions with a Personal Assertion

A personal assertion is simply a confirmation of actuality that is written out in a positive form as though the committed action has already taken place. This is personal, like your potential, only to you. Initiating this personal assertion also creates accountability. Making you responsible for the actions that you alone put into this assertion.

Let's go back to making this a personal assertion. Think about that. Only we can affirm any actions for ourselves. We can't affirm for someone else to do it for us. I am sure you understand by now that all intended actions must come from within, then out. Life is an inside-out experience. We think it (what we want), we feel it (why we want it), decide on what actions (how we will accomplish what we want), then finally we do it. The first three, what, why, and how are all inner drive functions, it is when we do it, that signifies to our outer drive for the committed actions we take.

Step 2 - We Need to Visualize Our Actions

When we are writing out our personal assertion, it is also a wonderful opportunity to visualize our committed actions. It's like this, we need to visualize and experience actions in our mind, then visualize the accomplishments regarding the end results that are considered those outer drive actions to be completed. It's also important to see yourself actively involved in the committed actions to be taken. Don't understate the importance of the proposed actions to be taken.

Have a clear picture of the result you wish to experience before you have taken the appropriate outer drive actions. In other words, what you want to do is see yourself accomplishing the results of your actions and feeling the joy and satisfaction of completing those accomplishments.

Step 3 - Emotions of the Heart

Okay, we have a written personal assertion, we have visualized our actions, now this step brings in our heart of passion toward the actions we will need to take. The inner drive of the heart responds to emotional feelings more than the words we may speak. As we want to go beyond mere feelings to the emotions of the heart, the more emotion we can put before the proposed outer drive actions, and the greater opportunity of success. It will be these strong emotions of heart that will be focused upon the actions needed to be completed.

Step 4 - Stop the Trying and Start the Doing

The previous three-steps are critical to your success for when you take your outer drive physical actions. These steps must be done effectively. In other words, we must take these steps seriously if we want to experience effective learning and growing from our reflections. Now, it's the most important step. This step includes the doing, or the compelling actions that must be completed.

What must we do to be effective? We must stop trying and start doing. In other words, the statement of 'I will try my best' is not good enough. I am sure this is a statement most of us have made at one time or another. It's another way of saying, 'I will work at having the right attitude and I'll work at the task, but I won't take full responsibility for the outcome.' (This is especially true if the actions are not completed effectively.) But is trying to do your best enough for a life of successful actions?

In truth, the feeling of trying alone does not communicate true commitment. It's only a halfhearted effort. It's not a pledge to do what's necessary to achieve the actions that are necessary to be effective regarding your reflective experiences. Think about it. Trying rarely achieves effective and successful outer drive actions.

So, if trying is not good enough, then what is? What's best is an attitude of doing and doing whatever we do effectively and completely. There is an enormous magic in the two-letter word of – do. When we tell ourselves, 'I will do it' we then unleash great power. That act forges in us a chain of personal responsibility that ups our game. It's a strong desire to excel, plus a sense of duty. It's a personal responsibility that belongs to us. This emotional inner drive motivates us to an all-embracing passion and dedication to getting done what needs to be done.

We have discussed our 'what we want', or our desires and 'why we it must have it', or our reasons, and the foundation as to 'how', or path we are going to take to get what we want. In addition, we have discussed those key questions, we must ask before acting upon them. And lastly, it's the 'how'. It's how we create the path and follow it regarding proposed actions we need to take. With this in mind, we now need the focused areas of discipline, motivation, and encouragement as to 'how' we will answer the call to begin our proposed actions.

Actions Requires Discipline

These proposed actions that are continually referred to throughout our inner drive process, will require us to be disciplined. Being disciplined is an inner drive function. First discipline, then action, and by the way, you will be required to perform more discipline while you're acting. So, be disciplined to act.

To create discipline, you must act daily and be intentional regarding effective reflection efforts. These efforts will spark repeatedly, embracing the intended learning to enrich your life. It is this enrichment that leads to your personal potential.

It's true that the reflective experiences of yesterday motivates your discipline today, and discipline each day maximizes your actions you made yesterday. That is a powerful statement requiring significant efforts and focus – or *intentional intentions*. Being intentionally disciplined will result in successful committed actions.

Then, as I previously stated, you must also be disciplined while taking committed actions upon your life each day if you are to live a life that moves you closer to fulfillment and personal potential. As reflecting requires deep thoughts and focus of our inner drive, it will be the intentional responses from your heart that initiate outer drive action steps. The results of disciplined and effective actions will help in creating personal growth.

Discipline Requires Motivation and Encouragement

And where does this motivation and encouragement come from? It is within all of us through our hearts as an inner drive function, just as our discipline. I am a big believer of both motivation and encouragement. I will also warn you that when it comes to personal growth, motivation and encouragement will get you started, but it is discipline that keeps you growing. So, really all three of these inner drive functions work together. If you want to grow, consistency of implementing these three functions are the key.

Your future is dependent upon your committed actions to grow. Learning daily guarantees you a future filled with possibilities of growth. It is when you are disciplined to expand yourself, you expand your opportunities, you move closer to your personal potential.

With that we are focusing upon our inner drive of the heart, let's go into some detail regarding how our heart responds to life's experiences and how they affect our necessary actions that are linked to three examples of losing something or someone and how the component of love is involved.

I honestly believe that it is not our mind, but our hearts that guide us in making many of our life decisions, or actions that are necessary for an effective life of learning and growing toward our personal potential.

Example One: Losing is a Part of Life

Life is filled with both winning and losing. As in the case of our inner drive of the heart, we also know how unfortunate things affect our heart. Why are we discussing this? And what does our heart have to do with our actions? It is because our heart can be affected by a *losing* situation, which then leads to affecting our actions we take.

For instance, when we win there is usually some type of celebration involved. We all love winning and want to repeat it often, but it is when we come up short, or on the losing end of something that most often our emotions turn to sadness and despair. When we have emotions of sadness and despair, these feelings are shown by the actions we take.

But there is hope. We all must understand that sometimes losing is also meant for us to be more self-aware and hopefully learn something from the negative experience. I have the belief that we can find something positive even in the most difficult situations. Think positive. Be positive. So, in other words, we are focused upon changing a negative experience into a positive one.

It is a reality that when we are occupied by reflective experiences, it's not always about winning in life – there are also times of losing. Yes, there are times we reflect upon these losing events or situations that we experience. For instance, if you look at your life, you will find occasions whereas you have lost something or someone close. You have a choice to look at these events as positive or negative. Choosing to look for something positive, even in the most challenging times, can help you personally grow from them.

For example, playing on the losing end of a relationship affects us emotionally within our hearts. It is the choice we make that will decide on whether we stay in turmoil or move forward in life. Again, while in deep reflection, we all have choices. Some of us move on, while others unfortunately stay emotionally hurt within; thus, buried in time with a damaged heart. Like it or not, we all have experienced what it feels like to be on the losing end of a situation, event, and especially in relationships. For many of us, these relationships can end in damaging our hearts and taking a long time for the mending process to heal us completely. On the losing end of anything can be one of the most difficult experiences in life.

As we reflect upon these difficult experiences, a loss not only floods our mind with despair, but also affects the heart. When our heart is broken, our tendency is to create barriers to isolate ourselves from further hurt. This is especially true when it relates to someone we genuinely loved and cared about. Now, imagine how these difficult circumstances affect our actions to attempt to learn and grow from our reflective experiences.

Responses are always tough relating to losing anything in life. To be on the losing end of anything in life is difficult; especially when it affects the heart. The hurt we feel can only be repaired by learning from the experience through deep reflection and making a choice to let go – freeing our heart in taking appropriate actions to move us forward. It is at this crucial moment that the choice of taking positive actions are so important. Further, selecting a positive attitude during these unfortunate times and not staying on the losing end of an emotional grip – to rise above – opens us up to learning and growth from these most difficult experiences. This all-important choice is discovered while reflecting regarding any negative situation or event. This essential inner drive reflection phase takes patience and time to develop the process of taking appropriate actions in the mending of our hearts so that we can learn and grow from the experience.

Example Two: Loving Life is Shown by Our Actions

As reflective experiences go, we can go from losing something or someone as in the previous example, or we can go to simply loving our life. It is always more pleasant when our reflections turn to all things that we are currently enjoying in life. This enjoyment is shown by our actions.

Reflection should attempt to focus upon loving your life. A positive life is one that is loved by you. Love is a reflection from the heart. To genuinely love life, we must begin with the right attitude. No matter the circumstances that life presents, our focus is our choice. It is that simple. It starts with a choice in choosing to love life. In choosing to love your life, you must be purposeful. It may be difficult to implement and maintain but remember our attitude toward anything in life is also a choice.

In loving our life, responding to our reflective experiences then allows us to choose to be positive and not let the outside world decide who we will be, what we will think, how we will decide to feel, or how to act.

For example, a great question to ask ourselves during reflection would be: How do we know when we love the life we are living? It all starts with the way we think while in reflection. Once we have given thought to any reflection, we move to emotions. How we feel about the situation then moves us to responding with our inner drive of the heart regarding the reflective experiences that will be demonstrated by our outer drive actions.

So, how do you know you're loving your life with these actions? What can we expect? It's like this: We may smile for no reason throughout each day, we might have that extra spring in our step, or our spirit is continuously positive by our actions toward others. Words do no justice – it is a deep sense of emotion in our heart and a tremendous feeling that indicates we love our life by the actions we demonstrate.

It is something you cannot hide – nor even want to. We may need to search for love deep in our hearts but once we reflect upon this affection and engage ourselves completely, we can embrace loving our life. When we absolutely love our life, the actions we take are positive, effective, and complete to lead us to our personal potential of growth.

Example Three: One Word – Love

We end this chapter with the strongest emotion of the heart – love. There is no stronger emotion than love. Just to think or say the word 'love' will create different emotions for all of us individually. Love means something different to all of us. Love also has many levels. For instance – love can hurt, or love can heal. For love is one of the deepest emotions that affect our heart, especially during our reflective experiences.

As our thoughts and reflections of love surface, there are many diverse levels, forms, and ways to show love – both inner and outer drives are actively involved. We chase love, or love chases us. At one time or another throughout our life we have experienced reflections that have touched us at all the diverse levels and forms of love.

We all need love and love needs us. It starts with a strong reflection of loving ourselves then transcends to loving and being loved by others – it is a bond that can only be broken by those involved. The strongest love there is, is enduring love. If we want this type of love, it needs to be pursued with powerful efforts in trust, honesty, and displays with acts of kindness directly from the heart.

Most of us yearn to find this kind of enduring love. This everlasting love is sometimes hard to find, but if we focus upon our reflective experiences, we may discover that this kind of love might be already in our lives. How do we know this? Because our heart tells us. Create a purposeful call to action and go into deep reflection within your inner drive of the heart and you will find that enduring love you have been searching for. Once we find this enduring love, actions become more successful and rewarding.

In this chapter, we discussed the inner drive questions of the heart regarding desire and purpose. It is desire that asks the question of 'what do we want?' Then there is purpose, or reasons for 'why do we want it?' Once we answer these important inner drive questions of the heart, we can then move to the final question of 'how', or 'what path will we take to get what we want?' The 'how' or path is regarding our proposed actions we will want to take to complete the reflective experience to learn, grow, and move toward our personal potential.

What about meaning and purpose? No matter who you are, where you were born, where you live ... okay, you get the point ... you can always find meaning and purpose in life. Remember that meaning provides the spark to light your purpose. And when you discover your purpose, your meaning will keep it burning bright. There is only one place to get this powerful meaning and that is to ask your heart. Deep down, we all know that these answers regarding our purpose are there. We need only to initiate them. It is when we ask our heart, it will lead us to our meaning and purpose in life.

So, it's now time to go to the next step of answering that call to initiate demonstrative actions ... Let's move to the next chapter!

CHAPTER 7

TIME FOR ACTION

ANSWERING THE CALL TO TAKE ACTION

In the previous two chapters we focused upon our inner drive of thoughts, feelings, and the strong emotions of the heart. These inner drive functions must be complete before effective outer drive actions are possible. In other words, there is the call, or intent to do something, then there is a compelling urge to take outer drive actions. The question becomes, do we always answer that call to act? Let's find out together.

Frequently, and throughout the day we reflect upon our experiences. And because of these reflections, many times there is a call for action necessary. What exactly does this entail? This means that from our thoughts, feelings, and strong emotions of the heart regarding our experience, there is compelling evidence to proceed with an outer drive action. So, let's go back to the question: Do we always answer that call to act? Many of us do act, others don't bother. Another question might be: When is the right time for responding with actions after we reflect?

There is something behind the idea of time for action. We all ask ourselves questions regarding this time. For example: Are there any barriers regarding time when we have compelling evidence to act? Should we act immediately after our reflective experience? Should we wait? This chapter, and its contents, will answer those questions. It is all about a time for action. This 'time' I am referring to is all the functions involved regarding answering the call to act.

There is time and there is action. Two separate entities, but one must work with the other. Time for action is about establishing this resource of time to act upon our reflective experiences. Why time? Because we all reflect upon our time and how its best used in our world in which we live.

The best way to explain this process is: A time to act is answering the call after we reflect upon an experience that requires us to take action. Think in terms of answering a telephone call. Many of us answer immediately – we hear our phone ring; we answer on the first ring. There are some that let the phone ring a couple of times before we answer. Still others don't answer at all. Answering the call to act after a reflective experience is the same idea. There are occasions whereas immediate actions are required of us, some actions need a bit more planning before we act, then there are those of us that do nothing. And if we choose to do nothing, what are the results? As it relates to our reflections, the experiences we have; the results equates to no learning, nor growth, and we remain where we are in life. Stagnant. Unfortunately, many of us remain without new personal growth because we don't answer the call for life-changing actions.

But, with the first two options, we have the opportunity for learning and personal growth. So, in conjunction with the first two options, there is a compelling urge to act that has great possibilities: resulting in making considerable differences in our lives. The third option, there are no actions intended; at least for now, and maybe never resulting in – nothing really. We must act now if we are to make efforts in striving for our personal potential.

To learn and grow in life we must take effective actions. How do we define these effective actions? Effective actions are based upon demonstrated physical acts, not just a feeling, or an urge. Remember this: An action pursued after a reflective experience will not go anywhere unless you apply it. Think in these terms – we start with nothing. Pursuing an action without application, you end up where you started – with nothing.

Three Levels Regarding Actions

With our inner drive functions of thoughts, feelings, and emotions of the heart complete, we can now move to answering the call to act. But we must also realize there is more to do than just take an action. There may be additional decisions to make before we act upon our reflective experiences.

As we are now ready to take outer drive efforts regarding demonstrative actions, we are faced with more decisions by our inner focus. Again, there are three levels, and all are focused upon time: Level One – immediate action. Level Two – only after more development and planning, then action. Level Three – doing nothing, or indefinitely delaying any response from our reflective experiences.

We must decide as to what level of action is required. This process of decision-making is done within with our inner drive. For example, let's say we are focused to go back to school to reach a higher level of education. In this case we may choose Level Two, needing more planning to act. Answering the questions: What will I study? What will be my major? What courses are required for my chosen major? What is the cost? How long will the process take? And so on.

Yet another example of Level Two might be a change in priority. Shifting our priorities takes time. There may be more developing, or planning involved, but our actions are still intact to implement when it's the appropriate time. In other words, we know what needs to get done, we plan for it, and we act upon it to completion. In priorities, we may shift from an immediate action to moving to adjusting to yet another form of action, or different action altogether. If done effectively, this will take a detailed plan to be successful. These are all timed responses.

Let's take another example regarding relationships. How about a strained relationship. These kinds of situations lie heavy on our minds and hearts. What is the timing for answering this call to action? This could be immediate; Level One or Level Two, to take some time in planning. And yes. Unfortunately, many of us choose Level Three – doing nothing. Remember, by choosing Level Three, the hurt and disappointment only lingers regarding a damaged relationship experience. It's not going to go away on its own. (We will discuss much more in detail regarding relationships in Chapter 8 – Learning Leads to Growth – Part 1.)

Patience Regarding Time

We discussed patience in the previous chapter, but what does this have to do with our time? Wow! Patience and time really go together. I believe one of the most underrated areas of patience is regarding time. I also believe that 'time' is one of the biggest barriers regarding taking actions. Let's not miss the opportunity to focus upon our time as we take necessary actions from our reflective experiences.

Time is one of our most precious commodities in life, yet it is limited. You could say that we only have so much time. Most of us would say we waste a bit of it, others would admit they would like more of it. Time is still a limited resource. There will be some time wasted and even occasions of inefficiency, of course some challenges, but the goal should be focused upon patience and effectiveness especially while taking actions as we reflect upon our most important experiences. This patience in time before taking committed actions would be considered Level Two response. This is with the fact that patience will require us to wait, and then pause in developing some decisions based upon our proposed actions.

If our time is indeed that important, then we must improve our efforts regarding how we manage it. We, in fact, are the only ones responsible for directing the use and how we spend our time. Because we direct these aspects of time, then we can also use it to our own advantage. As we think and reflect upon how we use our time, we can be more self-aware and learn to use this limited resource in unlimited ways using patience as a focus while we take important actions.

Too Much Time Delay

There are times when we delay things in life. For example: Occupying too much time to take actions after we reflect upon an experience. What if these actions called for a Level One, immediate response? In this case, we know action is required but we purposely delay the actions. These delayed actions can be at a later date, or indefinitely. Level Three is much different than a Level Two response. By delaying indefinitely our compelling urges to act upon a reflective experience, we may be too late to take actions, thus no learning, nor growth occurs.

Is it because we think we are not up to the challenges of everyday life? Or is it that we always tend to procrastinate? Whatever the self-imposed excuse, time delays will only stop us from taking the necessary actions in attaining the things we want in life. These things we want in life are often the same things we know we must take actions upon.

To intentionally reflect each day is to organize our lives so that in turn, we can embrace and enhance them. By not responding with ability, we may delay necessary actions to be taken. The only delays we create in life are of our own doing – we initiate the choices we make – or not. There are many reasons for time delays. In truth, these so-called reasons are really just self-imposed excuses.

For example, one most common excuse is procrastination. This only means that 'someday' we plan to do what we stated we would do. Stop procrastinating, no more delays. In other words, that 'someday' is today! Why is it that we do not take the time or make excuses for not following through for the things we want or need in our life? The bottom line is that we delay things in our life even when there are no outstanding barriers stopping us from taking the necessary actions to move us forward in life.

Have you ever reflected upon: When will you do something important that is truly needed in your life? The reflective answer more times than not seems to be – someday. Why not today? What is holding you back? If the answer is that you are just not ready; then the next question would be: What is impeding you from moving forward with appropriate actions? These are great reflective questions that need to be answered if you are to learn and grow in life.

The easy response is to have no time delays, but that is not reality. This is an improvement area for many of us. Have you ever heard the statement about life being described as it's not a 'dress rehearsal'. Many of us have. We only have this one earthly life to live and there are no second chances. Delays in life are easily overcome by taking the first step – by not waiting but starting. It doesn't matter what you do, just do something – it's about taking some type of action. It all starts by thinking and reflecting differently from a hesitant *not ready* to a confident *let's go*. This confident response is a Level One, or immediate action. A *let's go* attitude gets us moving forward, with actions of our outer drive functions that completes the cycle of learning and growing from our reflective experiences.

Are you ready to go? In many cases, no one is ever completely ready. But I will also tell you that no one ever gets ready to take actions by just waiting. The fact is you get ready by starting. Again, as you reflect upon any situation that needs some type of necessary action, you need to move forward even if there are still a few missing pieces, start anyway. Just know there are inherent risks to all we do in life. No one ever got ahead by staying where they are. Take necessary risks to discover a whole new world through the demonstrated actions you take – with no time delays.

Time Allowance Before Action

When we stop and truly purposely pause for additional reflection after some experience, we are at Level Two. This process moves us to taking the necessary time to ensure we are effective throughout the proposed actions we want to take.

We must all allow ourselves time to think about our lives. This time I am referring to is our reflection time. Pausing throughout the day to ponder regarding our overall lives and how we are living them is extremely healthy and necessary to live an effective life. This again, is a process known as Level Two and would be considered an operative time for developing and planning our actions. Think about it in these terms: Intentionally developing and planning for actions with our inner drive before demonstrative outer drive definitive actions.

If it is not an immediate action required, we then focus upon planning for proposed actions. This can be a highly effective process for these actions to be completed after the reflective experience. Again, in our hurried lives, we must slow down before considering taking actions. When we hurry through things, the consequences of these actions are sometimes not what we wanted, nor expected. To take the time for reflection upon our life's experiences is something we all should do more often.

We are all busy, but why bypass the opportunity for better self-awareness to enhance our lives that reflecting allows us to experience? One great example of self-awareness is when we take the time to reflect upon past experiences. It is in reflection that we often examine past experiences; learning from them to create growth, thus a better future. If there is no allowance regarding time to reflect, we become stretched, overwhelmed and at times, lost. There are questions that need answering and thoughts that need to be reflected upon – we need the allowance of time to think about our life's experiences before our demonstrated actions.

For example, we need time to ourselves – it's healthy and necessary. Unfortunately, people will always be asking for our time, but they will also need to understand if we are not always available. When we are *always available* to others, we then spend too much time focusing on *have to's* and do not leave time for our own individual *want to's*.

Life, it seems, is turning into a nanosecond culture. Moving too fast to catch up at times. The results create a gap between where we are in reality and where we want to be. In other words, where we are is the contemplating stage, and where we want to be is the outer drive functions of demonstrated actions. One of the best options to fill this gap is to refocus and reflect upon the things that matter most by allowing the time to do them. Remember, we discussed a change in priorities. This may be a suitable time to refocus upon what's most important to you. In this Level Two stage of developing and planning, more effective actions are possible.

Time Allowances Measured

The impact upon one's life cannot be measured by how much we do, but by the time allowed to be effective in reaching for our personal potential in life. The key to accomplish enhancing our lives is to set aside an allowance of time each day to think and reflect upon two perspectives – a planned future and a reflective past.

A planned future is the ability to reflect upon and implement plans of actions that provide direction for the day resulting in growing our potential. Reflective past is the ability to revisit the past to gain a true perspective, enhanced self-awareness, and a better understanding of past experiences. Both planned future and reflective past experiences will take time to develop and would be considered Level Two responses. The answering of the call to act may take additional time to reflect upon. These allowances of time sets the stage for our actions to bring closure to some things from the past and an opening to many new learning opportunities into the future. Whether it is a planned future or reflective past, both need effective time allowed for better self-awareness and applied learning opportunities from our actions we have demonstrated.

Reflection upon opportunities regarding time is how we measure and manage it. Measuring time is how long it takes to get our priorities accomplished. Managing time is how we spend it getting our actions completed and not putting them off. The key is being proficient at both measuring and managing our time while in reflection. It is the results of both measuring and managing our time that we do not miss the opportunities of life-changing actions as they arise during our reflective experiences.

What About Opportunities in Time?

I have mentioned delays and allowances in time as they both affect our proposed actions. When we are not effective with the reflection time we have, we will miss opportunities. The opportunities I speak of are actions we should have made at the right moment in time. These are opportunities regarding our lessons that apply learning directly to our actions, resulting in enhancing the growth our lives.

Of course, we have all heard that some opportunities only come once in a lifetime – it's true. Are you willing to take that risk? And what if this risk is an opportunity that could change your circumstances in life? Let's go back to our response levels. Opportunities in time could be defined as Level One, Two, or Three. As in Level One, many times actions are immediate, or more time to plan as in Level Two, and then there are those opportunities missed completely by doing nothing as in a Level Three response.

Reflection of opportunities regarding time are most important. This is especially true as we age. Can you think and reflect upon an opportunity you passed on and did not take the required actions to achieve the proposed opportunity? I believe we all have examples we could share. Unfortunately, when we reflect upon these missed opportunities, it is then realized that there is no way to go back in time. We have all had these reflective thoughts cross our mind from time to time. When we do miss these opportunities, life can feel like a disappointment. The feeling of disappointment is because we waited for 'next time'. Remember Level Three, and that is doing nothing, or delaying our actions indefinitely. As we have already learned, opportunities come and go in life – and sometimes only once. When we reflect upon and then discover that opportunities will not wait for us, we learn that when they present themselves, we must sometimes take a risk to experience the possibilities of the actions that could change our lives.

Successful Results Regarding Opportunities

The most effective response to the end of any given day is – what actions did I take and what did I accomplish? If our focus and expectation for each day is to succeed; then we try to not waste a day. The key in living our life this way is to reflect upon successful results of the opportunities taken regarding our actions we seized throughout the day. Opportunities are the things we cannot afford to miss out on. Again, many of these opportunities may only come around once. The best way to describe these one-time opportunities is the extra effort to take actions of what we consciously know will not be there tomorrow.

To know when an opportunity arises, we simply need to listen to our inner drive of the heart. When this inner drive is reflected upon, we can identify compelling reasons for taking appropriate actions we know we must take. Of course, these new actions may result in taking some risk. In this case, it is vital to reflect upon our confidence level of risk knowing we can achieve what we are striving for. It is by this manner of reflecting that you can create and embrace an environment of confidence regarding new opportunities for compelling outer drive actions.

Special Moment Opportunities

One key area of answering the call to act is the timing of when opportunities arise that are considered the special moments in life. I believe it's also important to mention special moments as opportunities to take appropriate actions. These special moments that we reflect upon are many times one-time events, or firsts. It might be the first time we see our children as they are being born, our children's first day of school, or our first day at a new job – notice the key word in what comes to mind is *firsts* – those truly extraordinary events that only occur once because they are firsts.

What is the action here? It is in these moments that our actions must be focused upon. We also know this calls for Level One, or immediate action. The actions here require us to be completely self-aware. There are many great flashes in time to experience in life – they are all worth the effort to pause and reflect upon. Remember we will miss the meaningful moments when we do not pause and step back from our hectic schedules. The key is to truly reflect upon each moment and be completely self-aware to enjoy them as they unfold each day. The understanding here is that even the passing moments can provide the opportunity to act upon them. Taking appropriate actions during these moments are just as important as those actions you take after a lengthy session of reflecting and planning as you would for Level Two. The only difference is one is immediate, and the other is after careful planning. Both choices can be highly effective depending upon your reflective experiences.

Just hearing or reading the words 'special moment', our first initial response should be excitement. It is with excitement that comes passionate outer drive actions. Excitement comes to mind if we think and reflect upon the extraordinary moments that we have experienced and connected upon in our life thus far. Note that I stated, *thus far*. I state this because there are many more to experience and connect with. We are all guilty of missing a few important moments in life. This is partially because we are too focused on the *next moment* to act upon and in turn totally miss the important ones – many of which are in the present. It's vitally important for us to try to not miss one.

It is when we miss these special moments and the opportunity to act upon them, that we lose any possibility of learning, nor growth from these experiences. It is in answering the call with appropriate actions immediately after these sometimes, one-time events, which have the greatest possibility to change your life. Are you willing to risk not taking the necessary actions?

The truth is, with each moment of reflection we should experience excitement, and in many cases, these are the opportunities of learning experiences. If we focus on the emotion of excitement, we are more alert and self-aware of the experience we are reflecting upon. These moments are the common thread of life; thus, we should make every opportunity to really experience and then reflect upon them. To accomplish this, we need to embrace each moment as it unfolds. The results of our efforts in answering this call to action then become the special moments left in our mind, held in our heart, and with us to reflect upon for a lifetime.

Challenged by Time

Answering the call is taking the required actions regarding our reflective experiences at the right time, the right place, and for the right reasons. If you remember previously in this chapter, we discussed certain levels regarding answering the call to act. Level Three was to do nothing, in other words, basically *hanging up* the call. It is when we *hang-up*, that we remain where we are in life – no learning, nor growth. This level is also a choice we are making. It is what I refer to as – challenged by time.

As already mentioned, just to take a few minutes out of your day to pause and reflect upon it, is extremely healthy and well worth the time it takes to do it effectively. If you are not effective in taking the necessary time to pause throughout the day, you will feel challenged regarding your time and not be fully self-aware while in reflection. Taking the necessary time to reflect is so important before the proposed actions are taken. It is when we don't take the time and effort to reflect that our actions may result in undesirable consequences.

Time flies! I am not telling you something you do not already know – we live in a fast-paced world. If someone told us that we needed to pause and reflect a few times throughout the day, most of us would have a difficult *time* with it and feel emotionally challenged by it. To pause and reflect each day takes a lot of emotional energy within. As we allow the necessary inner drive feelings and responses to begin, we then plan the actions needed after our reflective experiences. These inner drive feelings, and seemingly obligatory responses, can create challenges that put barriers in front of us delaying the necessary outer drive actions we know we must take. This delayed reaction is an example of being challenged by our time. It is when we purposely delay our actions indefinitely, or a Level Three response, that there is little likelihood of learning, nor growth when we are challenged by our time and how we use it.

Challenged by Time and Situation

There will be occasions in life that challenge our emotional health. In this situation, actions may be affected by our emotional response regarding a difficult experience. So, not only are we challenged by our time we have, but at times it may be the difficult situation involved.

Both of life's joys and challenges occur all around us daily. Do you take the time to pause and reflect after each experience? Those that do, learn and grow from them. Life's challenges can be simply initiated by the time it takes to reflect or be the result of some difficult event or situation you experienced. Learn to pause and address all the challenges it brings with attempting to reflect upon your life. Why? Because it is our life's challenges that are ones to learn by, not because they were difficult, but as to teach us what we can do better in the future when these same challenges or even different ones come before us. Understand that there are plenty of these challenges along the way –

just be aware and well-prepared to face them. How do we face them? Simple. With effective and immediate actions. Yes. These are Level One actions. They call for 'right now' actions to put resolution into our most difficult situations.

Challenges can be difficult and bring us down if we allow them to. The key is to always attempt to reflect upon the positive events in life, for they are the ones we hold on to close to our hearts. Hopefully, as we reflect throughout the day, there are many more positive experiences to smile about rather than any negative, or difficult situations that challenges us in some way.

Time for a Follow-Up Call

As I have mentioned throughout this chapter, taking the time to pause and then reflect upon an experience, will result in the most effective actions taken. So, once these actions are taken, now what? Once we take appropriate actions, the results of those actions must be reviewed and reexamined. This is what I refer to as the follow-up, or the *second call to action*. This initiating of a *second call* to follow-up, is to review how effective your actions have been not with just one experience, but all experiences throughout the day. Yes, this *second call* should be completed each time an action is taken. Additionally, these *second calls* are perfect for providing additional learning opportunities, especially if the results of our actions require more or different actions.

Although we all consciously or unconsciously reflect upon experiences as they unfold, it is also best to take the time to truly pause for deep, effective reflection of the experiences and actions you have taken for the entire day. This way you will experience the most effective learning from each event to help you be more self-aware to enhance the learning and growing stages of your life.

For example, when I reflect upon the previous days' experiences, I personally find it is best early in the morning. Why is this? It is because often it is our sleeping hours that we continue to reflect upon our experiences from our days' experiences. So, as a result, these reflections are still fresh in your mind as you wake the next morning.

Whatever time you choose to reflect, it will take approximately 20 minutes to pause and reflect upon the actions of yesterday. As we can be disciplined to do this each day, this *follow-up call* will ensure we are taking the necessary and effective actions after each experience. By just taking the time to reflect upon these experiences begins the process of acting. Again, by initiating reflection daily, you create a discipline for yourself. It is a discipline that will improve the quality of your demonstrated actions to therefore learn and grow from them. If we do not take the time and effort to do our pausing and reflecting after each experience, we can miss out on the significance of the actions we complete. When we take not only the time to reflect upon these experiences, but take the appropriate and positive actions, they will move us closer to our personal potential.

Answering the Call – Steps to Demonstrative Actions

1. Be present and self-aware in answering the calls to action.

2. Be patient as you demonstrate your actions to be effective in completing them.

3. Understand actions can be immediate, (Level One) or may need more time to develop a plan, (Level Two) or your call can be delayed indefinitely (Level Three). Remember, Level Three is not recommended if learning and growing is

the goal. It is acting upon our reflective experiences that makes the difference.

4. You can't act by waiting, the only way to act is by starting. After you have reflected, planned for actions, now is the time to demonstrate those actions.

5. Be aware of how important your timing is regarding answering your calls to act. Whether it be time delays, allowances, opportunities, or challenges regarding our time, we must take appropriate actions when called upon.

6. Follow-up. (Remember, we also discussed follow-up in Chapter 4 as it related to taking responsibility.) It's vital that after our actions are completed, to reflect upon those actions once again with our inner drive of thoughts, feelings, and emotions of the heart and review our results. Doing this provides possible additional learning and growth opportunities.

Now that you have read the previous chapters regarding your inner drive of thoughts, feelings, and strong emotions of the heart, we now begin the process of answering the call to action. It is in this chapter regarding answering that call with demonstrated actions, we begin to understand that it is a combination of a process that includes both inner and outer drive functions that are required to be successful. This required process completes the cycle of thoughts, feelings, emotions of the heart moving us forward to committed actions that lead to learning and growth toward our personal potential.

We also discovered that 'time' is vitally important as to when you choose to act. It is when you reflect with your inner drive, that your outer drive can take the lead to complete the actions required to learn and grow from your reflective experiences. Think of it this way: A call for action begins within, and it is the answer to that call is then shown by demonstrative actions upon the outside.

CHAPTER 8

LEARNING LEADS TO GROWTH

PART 1 – RELATIONSHIPS

I can't think of a better place to start other than the learning and growing possibilities regarding our people relationships. In fact, as we reflect upon our lives thus far, we will discover the many lessons we have learned, others often repeated, and still others, we are still learning from as they relate to our relationship experiences. The ones we learned by; growth occurred. Ones repeated, well, it may have taken us a few tries to honestly learn anything from these relationship experiences. But none the less, personal growth resulted from these relationship experiences.

So, let's stop there for a moment. Doesn't it bring back memories of our relationships from the past, or even our current day realities? There could be several reasons for this emotional connection to our relationships, but why are we frequently reflecting upon our relationships? I believe one important reason for this frequency is because we spend so much time with others, it just makes sense that our relationships would be one of those areas that we need to work on from a perspective of learning and improving upon. And the results of learning and improving – you guessed it – personal growth.

Let's return to the idea regarding the importance of our memories regarding personal relationships. A question we may ask ourselves is: What did we learn from these relationships? Well, if we are honest with ourselves, we will discover that there were some relationships we refused to learn from, there were others we didn't understand the proposed learning opportunities, or maybe it was the wrong timing for one or both parties in the attempt to build a relationship.

I personally believe all these things; particularly regarding our relationships, that undeniable occurrences happen around us, happen to us, or happen within us, and that they all happen for a reason. These reasons, we may not always completely understand them, but there will be people that are and will be placed in our lives for a certain reason. It is from these relationships that we learn from that in turn, lead to growth. I also have the belief that for many of us, if we had the choice of areas to learn and grow from, we would most likely select our people relationships as an important place to start. I am sure if we reflected upon all our relationship experiences up to date, there would be many learning lessons that we could think about. And no doubt, we also grew from.

A good example of these type of learning lessons are linked to the failed relationships we have had on our journey. Whether it be refusing to learn, misunderstanding, or being emotionally unfit; these are all a part of our relationship experiences. As I stated earlier, much of our lives are spent with our relationships with others. So, in this chapter we will dedicate our efforts to all the lessons learned, sometimes repeated, and unfortunately, others with no learning at all regarding our relationships.

Whether it be positive lessons learned, or repeated, many times there was also growth. The examples of no learning from the relationships are many times the ones we had to repeat, therefore, believe it or not, we also somehow grew from. In fact, I am a firm believer that no matter the circumstances, we eventually grow from every relationship – whether it be a success or failure, it does not matter. Further, whatever the case of relationship learning opportunity, there are areas that can help us stay focused upon positive learning and growing from these relationship experiences.

Let's begin with learning. What is learning all about regarding a relationship? First, learning is an active process. We learn by doing. And what is the *doing*? Doing is action. What is a reflective experience without decisive action? Well, maybe it's just a thought, some kind of urge, or a feeling one might have about the possibilities relating to the reflective experiences. These are examples of simple responses. To go beyond reflecting, we are required to take compelling, decisive, and committed actions. This requirement begs us to initiate a deep, driving desire to learn. Now, we go beyond. We don't just stop at desires to learn. We must also have a vigorous determination to increase our growth as a result of these actions.

So, what does learning have to do with our relationships? I think a good place to begin would be looking at these so-called reasons regarding the proposed learning opportunities that relationships provide. These reasons again are refusing to learn, a limited or total misunderstanding regarding the proposed learning opportunities, and the idea of wrong timing.

Let's look at each scenario regarding refusal and limited or total misunderstanding as they relate to our relationships. In addition, let's take a look at what would be considered wrong timing regarding a relationship.

Refusing to Learn

First, let's take refusing to learn from the relationship experience. In this instance, many of us would just reflect upon the relationship and move on. So, wait a minute. Is this an effective way to respond? Not really. With this response, there was no lesson by refusing, or basically ignoring the possibilities to learn and therefore, no growth regarding the relationship. In fact, at times, some of us would even respond by blocking this relationship entirely from our minds in an attempt to just forget about it altogether. Does this work? Maybe for a short while, but it will continue to haunt us until we deal with the issues regarding the relationship. When there is refusal to learn regarding our relationships, we tend to repeat the same mistakes. Thus, we create a negative cycle of unsuccessful relationships.

Misunderstanding the Learning Opportunity

How about an example of when we didn't understand the proposed learning opportunity? Refusal is one thing, but misunderstanding is another. In this case regarding some misunderstanding in the relationship, it's not that we didn't want to learn from the experience, it's more that we didn't know how to learn from it. When we discover that we don't know how to do something, it is required experience that we need. Think about that for a moment. If learning is an active process of doing, then it is from our relationship experiences that we need to learn from. So, it only makes good logic, the more relationships, the more learning opportunities. Well, hopefully. That is only in a perfect world.

Go back to some of your first relationships. Did they always result in success? I bet not. As we continue to experience more relationships over time, we improve, we learn from them, we grow from them. Really? Well, that's what is supposed to transpire. The best avenue to learn is to reflect upon our relationships and the experiences that occurred along the way. This reflection time would be spent going over the events of the relationship experiences and identifying where *we* went wrong, what mistakes *we* made, what improvements *we* could have initiated, and so on. Note that I stated *we*. In relationships, it's always best to include the perspective concerning the other person involved, not to put blame, but to create better understanding of the bigger picture. It's an educational opportunity if you would.

Wrong Timing

Then there is the example of wrong timing. This is a tough one. How do we know when is the right time to learn from our reflective experiences regarding relationships? The timing sometimes is the most critical area of reflection. One of the most common areas of 'good' or 'bad' timing is linked to our emotional state. Maybe we are simply just not ready because we are emotionally unfit for a relationship. For example, maybe we are going through a period of unstable life events, or we have recently suffered a personal loss of some type.

Doesn't this hit home for many of us? Relationships come in a variety of different forms but are always developed by at least two people. No matter the personalities, differences, or personal values; all relationships are unique. Not one is the same. To have any kind of success, one must be physically, mentally, and spiritually fit for the possibilities of a relationship to result in realizations of learning, growing, and success.

Lessons Regarding People Relationships

As we reflect daily, it is our relationships, or people connections that are the subject of many of our reflective experiences. Why are our people connections so important? It is because the people in our lives that we build our most successful and influential associations with.

115

I believe it is not things, but people in our lives that make the true difference in how we live and define our lives. I also believe that we can honestly say that it is the learning lessons and personal growth that has happened along the way that helps us define our successes, and unfortunately, some failures regarding our relationships. But overall, I would like to think there are many more successes, or bonds than failures as they relate to our people connections. These bonds are so strong that we take them on our life's journey – these special people become a part of us, as we become a part of them. It is this emotional connection that creates the grounding that we search for in life. And, by the way, this relationship journey creates many life experiences that provide us learning and growing opportunities.

Imagine living a life without relationships. Most of us would be lost without those special people that support and love us. It is these special relationships that help us reach our accomplishments in life. It is because of these accomplishments that our relationships stay intact. It is when we don't take appropriate and committed actions that we experience problems regarding these relationships.

As we take different paths in life, we also meet many people along the way. Many of which we create lasting relationships and others will be short-lived because of the type of connection we had with these relationships. Long or short, we learn and grow from these relationships. When we reflect upon our lives, both good and bad relationships will surface. At times, especially regarding what we deem as 'bad' relationships that lies unresolved issues of not taking the necessary actions that made them *bad* in the first place. Further, it is from these *bad* relationships that all the three reasons are used – refusal to learn by them, not completely understanding them, and especially not the right timing for the relationships to grow. Many times, these types of relationships usually end with anger and bitterness that ultimately does harm to us.

It will be the 'good', healthy relationships that will create happiness and joy in our hearts as we fondly and frequently reflect upon these experiences. It is also these same *good* relationships that we took certain actions to keep them positive. Again, like long and short relationship journeys, we have had the opportunity to learn and grow from both negative and positive relationships. With that most of us would rather stick to a positive relationship, then those are the ones we should focus upon. Further, it will be the positive relationships that will have the best opportunity for growth and success.

Areas of Growth

From these opportunities, come questions: What are the areas that we can take a path to positive lessons? What must we initiate to keep our relationships solid and that helps us continue to create learning and growing from them?

Some of the most important areas regarding relationships are credibility, having a solid connection, valuing one another, possessing passion, and the willingness to forgive when we make mistakes in our relationships. We begin with the area of credibility.

Credibility is an Action

There is nothing like credibility to keep us humble and grounded. Having credibility; people count on us to follow through on what we stated we would do. This follow-through comes in the form of committed actions we demonstrate.

So, when we reflect upon examples of not coming through regarding promises made to others, it can bring about great self-awareness to apply learning from these reflective experiences. This example could be that we refused or did not understand what our role was and what actions we needed to take according to the characteristics of the relationship. It is through strong relationships that are built upon mutual reliability and credibility that are meaningful by those that are involved.

Reflection allows us to go deep within our hearts to test our character – one very important area is our credibility. Credibility is an example of character. Our character is who we are – a focus upon our actions, not just words. It is our character that begins within through reflecting upon self, then is shown by our actions on the outside for all to witness.

If we want to connect with people, credibility is key. To be credible is to have people trust in that what we say will have action behind it – for trust, as is our credibility, both are an integral part of our character. Again, it is who we are. And who we are is shown by the demonstrated actions we take.

In other words, the way we live our life should outweigh how we describe it. We cannot just talk about what we are going to do; we must take the actions that not only match our words but attempt, to go beyond them to be the utmost in trustworthiness and at the same time, demonstrating credibility. It will begin with our reflections upon our own character that will initiate the connection process regarding relationships with others.

While reflecting upon our character and how it affects our relationships, it is both credibility and trust that go together. These are vital qualities within a person that must be reflected upon. We start with questions while in reflection: If we cannot trust a person's word, are they credible in our mind? For most, the answer is no – it is only through a person's outer drive actions, not just their words that trust and credibility exists. Unfortunately, it is when we experience someone who is untrustworthy or has no credibility, that we learn the most about ourselves and the truth in others that we have relationships with.

Again, to achieve credibility is the combination of saying and most importantly, doing. It is the understanding that we must have both credibility and trust to be successful regarding our relationships with others. Let me repeat this important message – when it comes right down to it, credible people are not only consistent in words, but in outer drive actions as well. In other words, what we express verbally must match what we do physically. It is while we are reflecting upon our relationships, that we need to focus upon our own trustworthiness and credibility levels. It is when we exhibit these qualities that people acknowledge our efforts; thus, we grow from. When we reflect, are the moments in which we learn more about ourselves and the relationships we are in. What's the results of having trust and credibility with others? It is when others can trust that we will follow through on our promises, we also earn their respect.

Connecting by Doing

Remember, *doing* is an active process and before we can have good relationships with others in a positive way, we must connect with ourselves with a positive attitude. Part of learning about ourselves is our efforts to find a connection. This learning consists of what inner drive thoughts we have, our emotions of the heart, the values we choose, and the outer drive actions we take. So, first we must connect with ourselves. Connecting by *doing*. As for connecting with ourselves, it involves the act of reflection. That in itself is action taken.

What about connecting with self? Why is this so important? There is no point in attempting a relationship with another person until we have connected with ourselves first. When we are successful in connecting with ourselves while reflecting, we will see the world in a unique perspective and with a different set of eyes. It is through this process, we grow personally. It is this impact of different perspectives that can change a person to believe not only in themselves but also in others. So, when we connect with ourselves, we also learn more about ourselves. The result of this learning leads us to our individual personal growth.

Connecting with an Emotional Touch

If you have read my previous books, then you have already been introduced to how I relate to the use of the word *connecting*. In fact, we discussed connection in the first chapter. Let me explain a bit further. This *connection* is an emotional touch. What is this touch? This touch is a powerful act that we each have the opportunity to share through mutual trust, openness, encouragement, respect, and caring for another person.

These characteristics can only be recognized by the acts of *doing*. In fact, the only way a person can feel this touch is by *doing*. When we sincerely touch other people's lives, the connection goes deep into their hearts and becomes a part of them. Through the years, I have had the privilege of feeling this type of connection with many people. It is these same mutual connections that provide a powerful impact that helps us to believe in ourselves and others, to have hope, share love, and to overcome difficulties.

Connecting with Others

In this book, we are connecting to our self-awareness regarding the reflections we experience as we are planning for appropriate actions to be considered. Then once the compelling actions are taken, learning begins that leads us to overall growth. So, connecting with ourselves is vitally important as we strive for personal potential. And since this chapter relates to lessons learned through our relationships, then this idea of connecting to another is important for the success regarding our relationships.

We all have opportunities to connect to ourselves regarding all things in life. But it is connecting with people that we hold on to most. It will be reflecting upon our people connections that moves us from our learning of today, to growing for tomorrow regarding these relationships. When we connect to others, it begins through our words, but more importantly, through outer drive physical actions.

Further, deep, effective reflection is connecting with the right people, and learning and growing along the way. We experience these *right people* by the successes we experience in life. It is these same individuals that influence us to reach a higher personal potential than we would on our own. When we focus upon others and allow for how much they influence us while in reflection, we can then apply the learning that we experienced in leading us toward our personal potential in life.

Valuing Others is Shown by Actions

When I think of successful relationships, there are three vital components that come to mind – mutual trust, respect, and showing value to one another. We touched upon trust and credibility and how the results creates respect. Further, we understand that these components are not just words, they are outer drive actions that must be demonstrated so the other person feels the positive result of each one of these components. As we reflect upon our relationships with others, it's important to keep the components of trust and respect close within our hearts to create effective reflective experiences. These experiences are linked to our lives which are meant for learning lessons, thus personal growth.

So, if we want to value or to be valued by another, it's like trust, credibility, and respect – we must show it. The only way to show that you value someone is through your outer drive physical actions. It is when our actions show how much we value others that we begin to experience the positive results regarding these relationships.

The feeling of being valued or valuing another starts with what our inner drive thoughts contain. It is when we reflect upon valuing others that we can focus upon how important these relationships are in our lives. The results of placing value upon another person creates a positive environment whereas both parties feel calm and comfortable regarding the relationship. The wonderful thing about it is that when we feel valued, we share with this great feeling regarding all our relationships. Think about it. The only way to feel calmness and be comfortable is through the outer drive actions we provide for one another. It's not just me, it's not just you – it's about us.

Unfortunately, this concept is relatively easy to understand but, sometimes difficult to implement if we are not used to valuing others. Applying value regarding another is through our outer drive physical actions. As reflections start with our inner drive thoughts and feelings, it is the demonstrative outer drive of valuing another that only begins when we commit to the actions showing this value.

For example, when placing value on a person, we need to expect the best. In other words, we start by reflecting upon and assuming a person's intentions and motives are going to be sincere unless they prove to be otherwise. When we think, reflect upon, and personally feel these positive intentions, it also creates the emotions of the heart to be opened to begin the process of demonstrating outer drive actions in valuing others. And how are these intentions shown? Yes, you guessed it – only through our outer drive actions.

All responses can be projected as outer drive actions taken. So really any response can be deemed as an action. For example, if someone has just demonstrated how much they value a person and then is acknowledged by that person in the moment it occurs, the sincerity of the value can then be felt immediately. In this case, the acknowledgement becomes the action.

As it relates to our relationships, it is about understanding people, not just looking at their shortcomings. To better understand our relationships is to reflect upon them. Start by being open and not judging them – just value who they are.

When we place value on another person, it is all about the person. What does this accomplish? It demonstrates just how important they are to us. It is through our inner drive thoughts, feelings, then outer drive actions. It is then that we begin to understand and know how much we care and value our relationships. Further, it is when this care is demonstrated, that we look for the best in others, the abilities they have, and help them realize their personal potential. What a wonderful opportunity for both parties to realize and value one another's personal growth in the relationship.

Togetherness Through Passionate Actions

May it be reflective experiences upon peers at work or family members at home, is when you really think and reflect upon your lessons learned, personal growth, and successes in life. You will also discover that you needed others to help you accomplish your improved learning, growth opportunities, and the successes in your life. This discovery makes us mutually realize that in relationships, we need each other. The results of this kind of focus then becomes the connection between two people that creates an emotional touch, which then initiates a passionate bond. It is from both emotional touch and passionate, physical bonding that motivates us to grow in our relationships.

Being together with others has many benefits. One most important benefit is that when there are more people involved during important decisions to be made; different perspectives and ideas can be realized. The results of this process are so powerful regarding learning and growth potential that it positively changes our relationships with others. Why powerful? It is because we are putting passion into our relationships with others. We need each other, and that means putting the utmost passion into creating a solid partnership with one another.

Let's go further. By adding the components of a positive attitude and being happy in a relationship, we have the wonderful opportunity for success. By being positive and happy within, will be the result of the outer drive physical actions we exhibit to others. This puts a whole new aspect to relationships. People that we have a happy and effective connection with, will help us in moving forward with continuous learning, growing, and succeeding in life.

Have you ever sat down for a moment to think and reflect upon the people who have helped you to succeed in life? If you haven't, right now would be a good time to start. Creating happiness and togetherness with others are the first steps toward success. It's a combination of words and actions that make this success a reality.

No matter how accomplished or important we think we are; we need to remember, any level of prior success was not achieved alone, but rather the assistance of someone. In other words, we need people to succeed. Therefore, it is of vital importance to reflect upon how we can show them the value they represent to us, for without them, our higher level of learning, growing, and relationship successes would not be possible. When reflecting upon people in our lives, one thing is for certain about successful relationships. What is it? Remember, it is a sincere effort to demonstrate mutual trust, respect, and value for one another.

Successful togetherness is created by at least two people working together towards common goals in life. When you put two passionate people together, you combine knowledge, talents, and skills to initiate and produce beyond the learning and growing than what you could have done by yourself. It is when we reflect upon these special relationships that we discover just how important and valuable these people connections are in our lives.

Forgiveness is Shown by Our Actions

There will be occasions that we will make mistakes regarding our close relationships. When we do make mistakes, it is a perfect time to reflect upon forgiveness. If we go back to the some of our lessons learned by our mistakes, we must remember that these lessons can be the results of our refusal or not understanding something in the relationship. Forgiveness can work in both areas. One action is negative, the other is positive. Refusal will bring about more hurt and disheartenment because you are refusing to forgive yourself or another. On the other hand, if it is from a simple misunderstanding, forgiveness can be highly effective with no blaming, just forgiveness.

Let's face it, we all make mistakes and many of those mistakes are regarding our relationships with people. It is from these mistakes with others that we have the opportunity to learn and grow from the most. So, when someone makes a mistake involving your relationship; the best thing to do is to forgive them. And what about the fact that maybe we are the ones that made the mistake? When we do, it's best to forgive ourselves. Reflecting upon our mistakes is a great opportunity to learn by them. It is when we forgive ourselves and others that the process of applying learning from our unfortunate experiences takes hold.

It is vital that you reflect upon those relationships that have hurt you and find forgiveness in your heart to release the hurt within you.

Forgiveness can only be provided through an act of love by the heart. This deep emotion of love will provide the foundation of forgiving one another. And when the process of forgiveness is provided, personal growth ensues.

There is no doubt forgiveness is sometimes difficult to extend to someone who has hurt us in the past; but to move forward, we need to forgive. If we don't find it in our hearts to forgive, the hurt will always stay with us and as we reflect upon these broken relationships, and it will only continue to affect us in a negative way.

Life is not always forgiving. From time to time, we all have been hurt in some way by the people in our lives. The problem is, if we continue to hold on to the feeling of hurt, we create a continuous cycle of pain and despair – for what we allow, we also accept. Reflecting upon forgiveness is truly regarding the learning and growth that you want to keep close to your heart.

We possess the power to overcome the hurt that was the result of someone close to you. We can break the negative cycle by going deep into our inner drive of thoughts and reflecting within, thus learning to forgive from the emotions of the heart. After all, forgiveness is not for those that have hurt you, it is about you. It is when you forgive another, you release the hurt that you are holding on to. Again, as a result of these actions, you personally grow from it.

We all have heard stories from other relationships and how they spent years reflecting upon the pain and despair from those that they allowed to hurt them. What stops them from moving forward? Why would anyone want to hurt repeatedly? What stops people is the refusal to forgive those that hurt them. This hurt and despair does not have to linger.

If you have the courage to forgive, then you also have the ability to release the resentment and judgment, thus overcoming the pain and moving forward in life. And the results? Learning and growing along the way and enjoying greater happiness in your life. Again, the most effective way to release this pain is to reflect upon forgiving yourself and others that may have hurt you. Just by reflecting upon what happened, why it happened, and learning from these difficult experiences, that the forgiveness process begins to heal you.

Forgiving is the first step toward recovery. Once you forgive, it will be by demonstrating responsive actions of compassion that will create more joy and happiness in your life – not just thinking about it but doing something about it through the necessary actions you take.

These examples of learning lessons regarding our relationships with our people connections should recall many memories of your own that may have needed some decisive outer drive actions to be taken. Be it refusing to act, or not completely understanding the situation, even the right timing, or just not emotionally fit, are all reasons for not taking outer drive actions when they were necessary.

But we need to go beyond merely reflecting upon these experiences. We need to ask ourselves: Are these reasons or are they really just excuses? For example, if we refuse or don't appear to understand. Are these just excuses to not move forward in life? Whether reasons or excuses, we need to push forward for learning and growing purposes.

Hopefully by reading the examples regarding growth areas of using credibility, connecting with yourself and others, valuing others, providing passion, and forgiveness, will result in continued learning and growing regarding outer drive actions. It will be these outer drive actions that will improve your current relationships and limit mistakes in the future. Remember, it is our learning that leads to growing.

View it as this – some changes may look negative on the surface, but you will soon realize that space is being created in your life for something new to emerge. That something is growth.

CHAPTER 9

LEARNING LEADS TO GROWTH

PART 2 – LESSONS LEARNED IN LIFE

In this chapter, we will dive into more detail regarding life's lessons. In Part 1 we discussed relationships as they will always provide great opportunities regarding learning and growth. As we move now to another phase of learning, we must remember to be open and embrace the tremendous opportunities that we have to learn from our everyday lessons in life. So, let's now journey into how these lessons in life lead us to personal growth. Personal growth. The only way for personal growth to occur is from a lesson that is learned and applied. But note, the lesson comes before the learning takes place. Why? Unfortunately, we don't always learn right away from our lessons. Lessons are just another way to look at our life's experiences. In other words, as we *experience our experiences*, learning is the intended outcome.

As you read and reflect upon this chapter, hopefully many inner drive thoughts and feelings will be inspired by just knowing that your life's experiences are truly a series of lessons that you have learned thus far. *Thus far*, you say. Yes! Thus far because there are many more lessons for you to discover. The point here is to understand that it is when we continually experience lessons learned that personal growth begins to take shape.

As in the previous chapter regarding our relationships, along the way, we will indeed have many experiences, make mistakes, and have distinct phases and paths that we follow. Along this journey, we will be asking ourselves several questions that many will be answered, others will not. These are questions like: Why did I pause to act when I knew the situation needed me to do something immediately? Knowing my life would change for the better, why did I ignore that action I should have completed? And why do I beat myself up over mistakes I have made in my life? The questions regarding these experiences that cannot be answered, we have the options of asking more questions or just accept that there may be no answers – at least right now.

Lessons Learned by Our Mistakes

Let's go back to the mistakes for a moment. We know mistakes are a common fact of life. We are not perfect. Mistakes are meant to be an integral part of life. With that we are focusing upon lessons learned, it is these unfortunate experiences whereas mistakes have been made, that we have the wonderful opportunity to learn and grow from. So, think in these terms: Although mistakes are not what we want for an outcome, it's really more comparative to experiencing a negative experience, and then having a positive result. So, even though we make mistakes, we can also learn by them. If you have learned nothing else while reflecting upon these experiences, you now have a better understanding and enhanced self-awareness that life is a continuous opportunity to create lesson after lesson.

The more lessons learned; the more personal growth is realized. In other words, we are always attempting to move forward, regardless of our mistakes, continuously pushing toward our personal potential. Why? Because the ultimate goal is to have learned from each lesson.

Phases Effect Lessons Learned

All paths lead to phases in life. As we discussed paths in an earlier chapter, each of these paths we take is a different phase. Along the way during these phases, there are many opportunities for lessons to be learned and embraced. It is each phase, or path we take that we have an opportunity to learn more about ourselves and the lives we are currently leading.

Have you ever reflected upon the phases of your life? Many of us have. It might be a certain path we took or a situation we were locked into for some amount of time, but these experiences were all part of our life phases just the same. The phases of life come and go while reflecting upon our life. We all experience both positive and negative phases in life. And you guessed it, we experience lessons along the way. How would we describe what these phases represent? Well, for one thing, all phases are unique in different magnitudes and lengths of time. The point regarding phases is that they do not last forever. In other words, the time spent is neither subject to timeframes nor parameters. But it is from reflecting upon each phase that provides the foundation regarding good lessons for personal growth.

There are desirable and undesirable phases in life. Of course, it is our hope that the undesirable phases conclude quickly. In fact, I would have to venture that most of us would rather just forget these negative events all together. Undesirable phases include hardships and challenging times such as financial problems, relationship issues, or health concerns.

I might ask, how do most of us respond to these challenging times? Unfortunately, many of us refuse to accept these realities. But what if we were to think differently? If we reflect upon these undesirable circumstances with a different perspective, it will be during these phases of adversities that we have had the potential for many lessons

131

to be learned. Again, the promising part regarding undesirable phases is they do not last forever – they are just temporary setbacks. Further, with the perspective of undesirable phases as being temporary setbacks, there is hope, there is a new outlook that these difficult periods of your life will pass, and you will be soon moving forward to a more positive phase.

Reflecting upon our lives, as I have mentioned, some phases in life we cannot wait to abandon. There are also a few that will cause us a difficult time letting go. Again, how do we respond? Many of us don't handle these situations well. It is reflections involving difficult phases in life that are time-consuming and difficult to go through both physically and emotionally. The problem is that they can consume us. The key is to reflect upon the lessons learned from each phase, be more self-aware, and to emerge a better person. Life is learning – learning is life, and phases are just a part of it.

Obstacles to Lessons Learned

There are obstacles all throughout the cycles of inner thoughts, feelings, and emotions of the heart. What comes next is the foundation of outer drive responses that are intended for us to learn and grow. I believe you may have noted that there are various barriers and obstacles all along the way from our reflective thoughts to our completed actions.

As we are discussing lessons learned, we earlier mentioned the fact that it sometimes takes a few experiences before lessons are learned. Why is this? It is because there are many times obstacles that we must attend to. Who has lived their life without obstacles? The answer is no one. It is the obstacles in life that make us think and reflect upon creating different avenues to avoid self-imposed obstacles and to be more self-aware of some of the uncontrolled barriers as they present themselves throughout our life's journey. What are considered uncontrollable barriers? It might be health issues, job loss, or an unforeseen financial misfortune.

There are many obstacles and barriers in our path. For example, reflections upon the past will always reveal the obstacles that we had to face during difficult situations or events. Reflecting upon our obstacles are life's reminders that our journey through it is not always easy. As we reflect, obstacles will get in the way of developing positive connections with our reflections. It is by our choices that allow these obstacles to remain stuck. To move forward, we must reflect upon solutions by identifying first; what are the impediments, then reflect upon the outer drive actions regarding our intentions to remove them. It is important to point out that it is making the choice to learn from these obstacles, that the lesson is applied, and better self-awareness and growth begins to take shape.

Unfortunately, through reflecting and focusing upon self-imposed barriers, we ourselves can be the obstacle. That is correct – we can be our own worst enemy by refusing to recognize the obstacles right in front of us. So, if there is a lesson to be learned, we are sometimes the obstacle, or gap between the experience, or lesson and the learning that is intended from it. Obstacles, if not faced, can paralyze us from moving forward in life. What are the results of being stuck in life? You guessed it – no learning, nor growth. We all have encountered obstacles that hold us back and prevent us from moving forward. The fact is, we need the courage to fill in these gaps, face them, then focus upon tenacity to remove them.

It's true that our own self-imposed obstacles have the potential to stop us in our tracks. It is through purposeful and positive reflection that these obstacles can be identified and overcome. At times, life seems to be one obstacle after another – we overcome one, only to move forward and face another. What's the reason for this? Well, it seems as though life is meant to be one lesson after another. And it is when we apply these life lessons, we learn by them; hence, personal growth is recognized.

We all need to appreciate that obstacles are part of life. Once we appreciate that obstacles are just a natural part of life, we can begin to think of them differently. In fact, many of us look at these challenges as a welcome part of life. Why? Because we know we can grow from them. With this type of positive reflective thinking, there are no surprises, for the expectation is that obstacles will naturally emerge on this path we call life. It is when we experience going beyond our reflective situations regarding the most difficult circumstances that we are focused to identify the gap between the lessons and our learning.

Knowing or expecting these obstacles will undoubtedly touch our lives, we must also arm ourselves with the combination of courage and tenacity while reflecting. With both courage and tenacity, they will provide us the confidence to confront and push forward despite the difficulties. However, if we take the negative path and give in to these obstacles, we will not move forward. The result is, we remain unsure about life, making it harder to power ourselves forward and live life to the fullest. We alone decide our own destiny in life and how we want to live it expecting that there will be obstacles along the way. It is these expectations that provide us with power. Power to go beyond our obstacles. It is when we move forward, despite the obstacles, that lessons are learned, and self-confidence is gained that results in moving us closer to personal growth.

'Becoming' is the Key to Lessons Learned

Once we can get beyond the obstacles; we can then focus upon our progress in life. This progress is continuous, or another way to think about it is that we are always in a constant focus of *becoming*. As we are always evolving, we are also *becoming*. This positive process of evolving is an endless series of life situations that lessons are learned and applied. Reflective experiences regarding *becoming* will always produce valuable lessons that will continue throughout your life's journey.

Let's look at this from another angle. Do you feel as though there are no remaining lessons to be learned? In other words, have you ever reflected upon life as you have now arrived, reached everything you wanted and all that you wished for? The word – arrived. Doesn't the thought of '*arriving*' sounds like the end of something, for we have reached our destination? Having thoughts such as this will only limit any future learning. Is this how you really feel? If so, it's time you think differently. What if, we started to deeply reflect upon and think of '*becoming*' rather than '*arriving*' and therefore not ending, but consistently transforming, to learn more, to grow more in life?

If you change your thinking, lessons in life will not have an ending. Further, your thoughts would believe that there is no such thing as a destination, and that life is a continuous journey of lessons. And yes, along the way, we learn from these lessons. *Becoming* is the continuous effort of being. In other words, as human beings, we are in a continuous state of developing into the person we are intended to become.

Again, life is a journey, not a destination. So, treat it as such. It is not about who we are today, but who we will become in the future, and beyond. It will be through reflecting upon your life that the idea of *becoming* will create not just a limited view, but more of a broader outlook on life. It's a continuous state of transformation. Life should be a focus of continuous learning, growing, and personal potential for we are always evolving.

To continue to learn and grow is to think and feel that life is always transforming or *becoming*. If we are to live a life of *becoming*, we must motivate ourselves to be in a continuous state of enhancing and embracing learning more about ourselves and how we live our lives today and beyond. When we embrace this type of inner drive thinking while reflecting, we look forward to each day with passion and excitement, and more of who we want to be and what we want in life.

A focus upon *becoming* creates a new beginning and it changes how we live and see the world. Remember that life is full of different phases. It is in these phases that we discover where we want to go and what we want to become. We should all reflect upon, embrace, and enjoy the journey. To go beyond reflecting regarding your life's experiences, you must be willing to never stop growing with the passion and commitment to be the best you are capable of *becoming*. Life is filled with things to see and do, so why not always focus upon continuous learning and growing? As we reflect and focus on this avenue of living our life, we will always have the focus that there are more lessons to be learned.

As we continued in this chapter to discuss the idea of learning leads to growth, we also discovered that along the way, we will experience many lessons to experience on our journey. And with these lessons, we begin to experience how this valuable learning leads to growth. Many of these experiences are complex and impact our lives in such a way that we refer to them as paths or phases. I believe the most important thing to remember about our phases, is that learning is continuous and personal growth is always an opportunity.

Of course, there will be obstacles in life. There will be good days and bad days. There will be wins and there will be losses. There will be successes and there will be failures, and sometimes life will be downright difficult. We will question ourselves and how we are living our lives during these challenging times. So, what should we do about it? We first must have the right learning attitude for the high times as well as the low times. It will come down to how we respond to these times that makes all the difference. Some of us will get stuck, while others will find a way around these obstacles. Many will continue to falter, still others will focus upon pushing these obstacles aside and experience the lessons and learning intended from them.

Lastly, the idea of 'becoming' and not 'arriving' is important to grasp. We are all on a journey of continuous life lessons to be learned. This journey does not stop for it is intended to be lifelong.

CHAPTER 10

OBSTACLES TO GROWTH

In Chapter 4, we discussed the barriers to act. Here in this chapter, the actions have taken place but there are still obstacles holding us back from growing. In Chapter 9, we discussed obstacles to learning. Shall I go on? As you can see, there seems to be a pattern developing. With each inner and outer drive function, whether it be before we act, as we attempt to learn, or even to grow for that matter, there will be gaps along the way. These gaps are teeming with barriers and obstacles that we must remove before we can fully realize any positive results as we strive for our personal potential.

Obstacles Begin with Beliefs

Going beyond obstacles for learning purposes is one thing, now we have to face more obstacles for growth? It will come down to how we emotionally respond to our reflective experiences. I believe, before we can move from turning learning responses into growth, we must discuss our personal beliefs within ourselves. These same beliefs control how we feel and act according to the *experiences we experience* during our reflective time. These same beliefs become obstacles to our growth if we allow them to get in the way of our forward progress in life.

Again, in the previous chapters, we discussed obstacles and how our thoughts can limit our learning capabilities, here we discover a common obstacle to our growth – emotional beliefs. I honestly believe there is an important link between the inner struggles, or obstacles regarding our efforts to take actions, learn, and even to grow from those actions. What are these inner struggles? It seems that our feelings are much to blame. As I just mentioned, I further believe that with pending obstacles to growth, they are somehow connected to beliefs, or our emotions. These beliefs and the obstacles that are attached to our beliefs are what commonly prevents us from acquiring our personal growth. And that, my friends, will be our focus in this chapter.

So, what are these growth beliefs? They are emotions, or feelings that are introduced after we have reflected upon our learning experiences and following the compelling actions attached to these experiences. And as I have stated, it is throughout these experiences that brings us barriers and obstacles. But one of the more difficult obstacles is to apply growth from our actions. So, the first question we might ask ourselves is: Do we believe in ourselves strongly enough that we can apply these actions into personal growth? The answer should be a confident – yes. But what stops us are emotional obstacles. These emotions gather within ourselves regarding self-belief, or self-imposed struggles. And imagine this, there are those that even believe nothing can bring them additional growth in life. If this is indeed true, it affects their teachability. Some emotions are linked to fears we have. And with fears, come worry which then brings on procrastination. It doesn't stop there. At times, our obstacles come from the outside – from our relationships with others that affect our emotional state. We will touch on all these obstacles throughout this chapter.

When you truly look at these beliefs, they are all self-imposed. The best part is that if these beliefs are indeed self-imposed, which also means that we have the total control to change them. Like in Chapter 4, we discovered that self-imposed barriers get in the way to act. Same here. The possible obstacles in moving forward toward compelling growth is our level of emotional strength that is in question. In this case, it's not what we think, it's how we feel. The truth is we can choose to grow anytime we emotionally desire if we just give up the belief that we can't do it. It's that simple.

Our life experiences lead us to believe certain things about ourselves. Whether these beliefs are true or not really doesn't matter because if we accept them as true, then they are then true for us. The problem, or obstacle stems from if we believe in these truths long enough, they become a part of us. If we allow them to be our life, that's all we know. Further, if we currently have these feelings, we will discover that personal growth will be exceedingly difficult for us to attain.

Once we have accepted this type of feeling, the only way to change it is to change our emotions. If we choose not to change our emotions by creating then our own limitation through our belief system, we stay where we are in life. We become limited not by reality, but by the reality we are emotionally perceiving it to be. What are the results of these negative realities? In short, growth is limited, or at times, nonexistent.

Shaking Free from Mistaken Beliefs

The fact of the matter is that we can only be successful to the degree that we are willing to shed our mistaken beliefs to reach our growing stages. When we feel stuck and experience failure, deficiency, or limitation, it's often because of the unconscious limitations of fears, worry, self-confidence, or from other people. The wonderful thing about these emotions is that we can change them if we choose to.

The sad thing is that even though we know our lives aren't working in certain areas, we are emotionally afraid to change. We stay locked in our comfort zone, no matter how self-destructive it may be. Yet, the only way to free ourselves from our problems and growth limitations is to allow ourselves to step beyond these mistaken, negative beliefs, and take appropriate actions to attain the personal growth we are striving for. Now, read that last sentence again.

This means after thoughts regarding our reflective experience, after actions to learn, then additional actions to grow – we then must take further actions to move beyond our barriers and obstacles. Wow! That's a lot of work! You bet it is! It is hard work, passion, and tenacity that makes the difference between those that apply actions to grow and those that don't want to do the work to have greater success in life. The fact remains that if you genuinely think about taking any actions to improve your life, they are all outside your comfort zone. And the only way you will ever create actions from your reflective experiences is by stepping out of your emotional comfort zone and be willing to continue to initiate those actions all throughout the reflective experience. This process creates the growth needed to strive for your personal potential.

Going back to some of our mistaken beliefs in ourselves, whether it's procrastination, fears, worry, or even negativity from others; they all can stop us from moving forward in life. It's important to remember that if we indeed believe that these emotions from the inside or someone from the outside create roadblocks, we will continue to look for excuses that we believe are out of our control.

In order to find the true answers or solutions to any problems, we must begin by taking actions and looking within ourselves with a new emotional attitude. It is with this new attitude that will cause us to see ourselves, our reflective experiences, and others in a new perspective.

Yet put another way, no amount of determination, no amount of willpower, influence, inspiration, or even motivation will solve our problems. That is if we continue to make self-imposed excuses for not taking decisive actions to change our lives; we will in turn, limit our journey toward personal growth.

Our Obstacles to Growth are Simply Just Struggles

How can the struggles of growth be stated as *simple* as this heading suggests? Could it be that we are the ones that create these so-called struggles? The answers are first, these growth struggles can be simplified and second, yes, in many instances we are the ones responsible for these growth struggles. Think about it. Let's stop right there – thinking. Remember that everything starts with our thoughts. Also remember in the previous chapters, our inner drive thoughts can be the obstacles to limiting our abilities to learn. If we allow these obstacles of negative thoughts for learning, then growth will not occur.

So, previously we discussed obstacles of learning limitations of our abilities regarding how we think. For growth potential, we move from our thoughts, to feelings, then to more emotions. These emotions can stop us or promote our growth. Like our thoughts and simple feelings, our emotions can also be reactionary. Reactionary emotions lead to bad decisions that create our own self-imposed struggles. In fact, many of us are our own worst enemies regarding our personal struggles. Yes! We tend to sabotage our own lives.

It's basically a matter of getting our mind right, our feelings in-check, and the rest is effectively responding to all of life's reflective experiences. But none of this occurs until you resolve your struggles. What about living life without these personal and emotional struggles? Is it even possible? It is only possible if we first, acknowledge, then reflect upon this notion, that a great number of us would finally admit that our struggles regarding the possibilities of personal growth are really just the emotional obstacles that lie within us.

Let's go deeper into the real problem of self-realization of our struggles. We will, in our lifetime, experience some natural struggles of personal pain and difficulties from external sources. But as already mentioned, one of the biggest obstacles comes from within and is staring back at us in the mirror. Yes, for the most part, we become our own struggles in striving for personal growth.

Struggles with Difficulties

I will also tell you that the journey of growth is not always filled with joy and happiness. In fact, by now most of us have come to realize that our life's journey actually includes those times of hardships, pain, illness, and all kinds of difficulties of one kind or another. This is real life. We are all subject to tough times, no one person is immune from these difficulties. Difficulties can come from all facets of life, but for the most part, many of these difficulties are external. In other words, they happen to us, and most times affect us negatively. But we also have the choice not to accept these difficulties. Why? Because we have the power to face them.

To face these difficulties head-on, we must reflect upon them. After reflecting, what we come to realize is that it appears as though that life wants us to be strong and grow, but no one can become strong to grow without struggles regarding adversity, resistance, and day-to-day problems.

So, what we discover is that it is these emotional struggles we all experience, are those that truly make us strong and promotes personal growth. If that is indeed true, it is also true that in the process of overcoming these struggles, we can still achieve our personal growth potential in life. In addition, as we gain strength from these difficult experiences, it is also an opportunity to learn from them. And the result of learning is growth. With these encouraging efforts, we learn thereby how, despite the struggles, life can be less complicated and more about a joyous and truly exciting adventure as we experience personal growth along the way.

Let's back-up for a moment. So, we are successful with the removing of difficulties through some reflection, what about our emotional struggles? How do they affect us? Unfortunately, many of us have given up on growth opportunities. And when this occurs, it's the opportunity to ask ourselves questions. One common question when difficulties arrives: Could it be possible that our life is not going in the direction we planned? I am sure we have all experienced undesirable times in our lives – or going sideways. How do you respond during these current challenging times? I would venture to say that most of us respond in an 'unhealthy' way that only makes matters worse and damages us emotionally and sometimes physically. What we discover is that these difficulties can prevent us from personal growth, but only if we allow them to.

There is another way – that is to respond to these unfortunate situations with a positive approach, for we truly have control over how we acknowledge and respond to life's experiences. No matter what the circumstances, we can choose to look at most situations with a sense of responsibility to learn and grow from them in some encouraging way. Life is a series of events – good and bad – it's really up to us as to how we respond to them.

Struggles with Decisions

Yet another common struggle is regarding decisions. Do you ever feel like you are making one bad decision after another? There is good news – you can change it. It is in how you approach life; especially in challenging times – bad decisions are just poor choices. It is only the good choices you make that builds upon effective growth. In fact, life can be one growth opportunity after another if you are intentionally creating choices to make it that way. It matters because you alone oversee your emotions. As these emotions are attached to our choices after our actions, then it only makes sense that we need to make good choices as we apply them to our growth potential.

Growth Setbacks

How about setbacks? Life is difficult at times. Let me repeat, life is sometimes difficult. Just striving for growth will, at times, form setbacks. Everyone experiences setbacks. We even discussed setbacks to learn in the previous chapter. Same here. There are setbacks to growth as well. But, when you have them frequently, as sometimes happens, they can be incredibly stressful and discouraging to face. If you allow them to be so, they can take the emotions of happiness right out of you. But you should also know that even though these growth setbacks can bring you down to your lowest point in life, you can always find ways to acknowledge these growth setbacks and push forward regardless of how difficult these setbacks may be.

It is only when you push forward, that you begin the process of turning these emotional setbacks into growth comebacks of enduring anything difficult that comes your way. Remember, most of our challenges, or struggles are self-imposed. The point is, we must endure, we must approach life in a positive manner if we are to produce personal growth.

It is when we approach life with more positive emotions that we recognize personal growth is possible. What we truly discover is strength within that; unless we experience these setbacks, we would have never realized how important these hindrances were to our life's journey.

Our Struggles Tested

Do you want to move beyond your struggles? Want to become stronger? Well, first we are tested regarding our struggles. As we have learned, most of these struggles come in the form of self-imposed emotional obstacles regarding our beliefs. Here are just a few: belief in yourself, teachability, procrastination, worry, fear, and negative people. Let's take a moment and look at a few of these self-imposed, limiting beliefs. We begin with belief in yourself.

Belief in Yourself

We introduced the chapter regarding our obstacles to growth begin with beliefs. Here, let's just focus upon our personal beliefs regarding our own individual emotional attitudes. Belief is another emotional attitude that begins within but shows up on the outside through responses to life's situations. Belief. Whatever you believe emotionally, becomes your reality. And this reality is shown to us on the outside. For example, if you respond to your life's experiences with a strong belief in yourself, it shows. Physically standing tall and confidence in your voice. To all that witness this, there is no question there is a strong self-confidence and personal belief attached to you.

Unfortunately, many of us don't want to believe what we see in ourselves because we have already made the decision to see what we want to see. Weird, right? But for some of us, it doesn't matter if the belief is true or not – it's in our heads. Like a negative response, it is our emotional belief in ourselves that begins with what we think about ourselves. On the other hand, having disbelief in ourselves, leaves us with false hopes and dreams. The bottom line is that it affects who we are, which also affects our growth potential. The problem exists that if we believe it in our minds long and intensely enough, it becomes our truth. Talk about complicating your life!

Everything that we believe today about ourselves, our relationships with others, and the world around us, have been learned or influenced from someone, someplace, on some occasion in life. Whatever the actual source, once we begin to believe it, it becomes our internal truth only because it is true for us. We must change this kind of attitude if we are to promote growth in our life. Our emotional attitudes begin with what we think of ourselves. The key to success: Simply stated in just three words – *believe in yourself.*

Again, simply believing in yourself is an attitude – a strong emotional positive attitude. Most of us would admit that we sometimes have doubts concerning ourselves – our abilities, relationships, or just our overall way of life. When we do, we stop short of our personal growth potential. If this feeling is allowed to persist, it will only cause limited growth and more complications in our lives.

Others can encourage or influence us, but our belief in ourselves comes from within. To believe in oneself, it starts with positive affirmations reminding yourself that you can do anything you set out to do. And when you do, the growth possibilities become endless. No outside obstacles can stop you if you just believe in yourself. If we learn to feel differently and truly recognize our strengths with a new attitude, we can then approach life completely believing in ourselves. What are results? You guessed it – personal growth.

Let's go further. Who are you? It is responses to our feelings that play a key role as to how we define ourselves. Why is this? It's our emotional attitude toward ourselves. If we really dig deep within, who we are becomes our own reality. Strongly feeling this way, our life truly becomes self-creative. So again, we are defined by these feelings. Then it only makes sense that we use life to create ourselves regarding our purpose as to who we want to be. Further, if we understand that we are indeed self-created, we can also respond by changing ourselves if the image we have of ourselves no longer reflects who we are.

Then there are those that allow others to 'tell' them who they are. It's unfortunate that many of us allow others to influence us this way. Remember that we choose. We can, at any time, free ourselves from feeling this way. Be self-creative. Be your own passion. Be your purpose. In fact, as mentioned in previous chapters, all three of these emotional attitudes of self-creativity, passion, and purpose, play a key role for our growth to occur. Never allow others to influence you to believe differently.

Having trouble finding this purpose and believing in yourself? Whatever the reason, you need to change it. You will never change your life without changing something you do daily. That change is created by producing significant efforts and developing strong habits – and that takes discipline. (We talked about discipline in Chapter 6.)

Discipline is a strong emotion. Discipline means if there is a gap between where you want to be and where you are today, then you need to fill that gap. You fill the gap by delivering daily efforts. It's these efforts that builds you up with an emotional attitude of belief in yourself. Giving effort not just for a day, but on a consistent basis. It is only then that you will change your life. In other words, efforts equate to actions, then to personal growth.

Fill-in the Gaps with Belief

Let's revisit these gaps for a moment. For example, as I shared, there are many occasions where a space or gap is formed between where we are currently and where we want to be in life. And remember that along the way these gaps will be filled with various barriers and obstacles that will be in the way of learning and growing. The understanding is to find ways to fill the spaces. How do we fill them? First, it's having belief in ourselves, then it truly comes down to the positive choices we make. Life is a series of choices. Positive choices lead to positive actions and it is these positive actions that you want to fill the gaps. These actions are responses to the choices you make daily. It is these same responses that lead to actions that then lead us to growth.

Too Much Belief

Is there such a thing? The short answer is – yes. Haven't you known some highly educated and successful people who don't want to grow? Some people feel as though they already know it all. Really? It is when we get too comfortable with our life that changing it becomes more difficult.

An example might be that we have the belief we don't need more personal growth, for we have already reached our own growth potential. Or maybe we are waiting for growth to come to us in some way. This couldn't be more wrong. Many of us get stuck in this comfort zone hoping that a different, more appealing circumstance will come along. Are you kidding? With these feelings, we don't realize how much we are hurting our potential. The only thing that can come between a person and the ability to learn and grow is one with an arrogant attitude. This kind of emotional attitude believes that they can no longer grow. In fact, they are unwilling to grow.

We have the choice to sit back and wait for something to happen or we can move forward with passion and purpose to grow in life. This decision is ours alone. Once we have made the choice to move forward to living a fuller, more joyful life, we can then begin to experience life in a different light of continuous personal growth.

Are You Teachable?

A good question to ask yourself is: Are you teachable? Why this question? Because how you answer this question you will need to be cautious for it could change how you feel about learning and growth. The best answer is to believe that we should always be learning, always be growing. Remember in the previous chapter, it's a lifelong journey with really no destination concerning learning, nor growth. Why is this? For success in life, continuous learning and growing are required.

For growth, one must be teachable. Teachable people are always open to innovative ideas and are willing to learn. They also know if they want to expand their growth, they must be open to acquire new knowledge, skills, and enhance their natural talents. Now, go back to those that think they know it all. Do you think this is possible? If you think you already know it all, there is no room to expand your mind, nor any possibilities of personal growth. The key is to think, then feel differently. If you don't have a teachable mind, nothing can help you change how you feel about continuous growth. How about this personal example:

As a professional life coach, I ask my potential clients a series of questions included on an introductory assessment that are answered by a simple – yes or no. I ask them to be honest with me, more importantly, be honest with themselves as they answer the questions on this assessment. Here are some of those questions:

o   Are you open to other people's ideas?
o   Do you listen more than you speak?
o   Are you open to changing your opinion based upon new information?
o   Do you admit when you are wrong or if you make a mistake?

- o   Do you observe before acting upon a situation?
- o   Are you willing to expose your inexperience if you are not sure about something?
- o   Are you willing to ask for direction if you need guidance?
- o   Are you open to doing things in a way you have not tried before?
- o   Do you learn more about yourself when given constructive feedback?
- o   Do you listen openly for facts when there is disagreement?

The results: If these potential clients answered 'no' to many of these questions, they no doubt have room to grow in the area of teachability. First, they may need to reexamine their attitude; then learn more about their humility. Being positive and open are the steps toward personal growth. And truly, our honesty goes both ways. If the potential client answers 'no' to many of these questions, I will be completely honest with them and share that they may not be ready for personal coaching.

'Someday'

Here is one of my favorites. It's called – *someday*. (We talked about 'someday' in Chapter 7 – Time for Action. Let's go further.) We all have halfheartedly stated that *someday* we want to be successful in life. But how serious were we? The problem with this question and how we answer it is that not everyone wants to take the necessary steps, or actions to get there. Most people make excuses like, 'Someday I'll work harder and get that promotion.' or 'Someday I'll start that weight-loss program and lose that extra weight that I have always wanted to lose.' Or how about this one: 'Someday I'll learn to be more productive by managing my time better.' As these questions relate to obstacles to growth, the time is now to create change in your life. The fact is, we can't wait for that *someday* to come along. Why? Because there is no better day than today to apply those compelling actions to promote growth today.

Procrastination

Another fancy word for 'someday' is called procrastination. Procrastination has a habit-forming array of factors involved that make it harder to move away from it. Here, procrastination is about purposefully waiting to apply actions you know that you must commit to if you want personal growth. These too, are self-imposed obstacles. Here are three of those factors. Can you identify with any of them?

1. *Lack of clarity.* If you're unclear about the actions you need to take, you will often end up barely beginning the actions to apply to your growth. But the problem is that you will not complete it because you are not sure if it's the right action to take.

2. *Lack of ambition.* How badly do you need to act? If you have to ask yourself that question, you do not have the motivation to do it. If you don't have a big enough reason for taking the actions you know you need to apply, you often never really get started at all regarding those actions for growth.

3. *Lack of priorities.* Like many people, your actions regarding important reflections lack priority. We go back to the 'someday syndrome' because we have not given our actions the proper priority.

Lack of clarity, ambition, and priorities are all focused upon how we feel about getting started and applying any necessary actions for our growth. The problem with the feeling of getting started, there is yet to be movement forward with any demonstrated actions. The results: no growth potential.

Fear to Grow

We touched on the emotion of fear in Chapter 4. Fear can stop us before we act and then again after the actions have taken place. Then there is additional fear waiting for us as we attempt to take those actions and apply them for growth. Why, and what is occurring? The 'why' is because there will be gaps all along the way: after reflection, before responding, after responding, before actions, after actions ... I think you get the point. The 'what' are the gaps of barriers and obstacles we must fill.

Let's go back to assumptions for a moment. We discussed assumptions in Chapter 4 and one of the biggest assumptions is fear. Yes. Fear! Just striving toward applying necessary actions to grow could be deemed as a sense of fear. So, what is the difference between those that want to go beyond their feelings to act upon them and those that are stopped in their tracks regarding barriers and obstacles?

Well, it's like this: Those that long to fill in these gaps of barriers and obstacles take necessary actions to confront their fears, move toward these fears, deals with them, and resolves any fears that come before them. Then there are those that remain stopped in their tracks, are just that. They are so afraid to move forward and not to mention, they also believe that they will have no success growing in life, so they do nothing to change their circumstances.

For those who want to grow and strive for their growth and personal potential, will choose to fill these gaps by confronting their fears to move forward. Sounds good, but how is this possible? Well, first; we must change. I have mentioned change previously. In order to grow in life, there must be change. For that fact, even change can be fearful but only if we allow it to be. It is when we move toward things that we fear that the seemingly daunting uncertainties appear to diminish in their assumed size and influence. Why? Because we are facing these emotional fears.

Unfortunately, many of us back away from these fears, and will avoid them altogether believing that maybe they will just go away or disappear by themselves! The problem is that this fear will only grow stronger and will take over our emotions and, by the way, will also limit our opportunity for personal growth to occur.

The truth is that we have the ability to do anything we focus upon if we work hard enough. Another truth – there are no real limits – only those that we place upon ourselves. These fears can be changed to positive challenges just by altering our emotions.

The key to success is to not allow fear to suppress your emotions. Fear can bring both denial and avoidance. With denial and avoidance, they can be a way of self-protection – especially when reflecting upon challenging times regarding the past. Another key is to not judge, just be honest with yourself. It is when you don't judge yourself that any pre-determined emotional fears can be released. And when we don't judge ourselves? What are we accomplishing? We are indeed confronting, dealing, and resolving our fears.

Fear Leads to Worry, Insecurity, and Uncertainty

Like mentioned in Chapter 4, assumptions can bring worry, insecurity, and uncertainty as we attempt to grow. Where do these feelings come from? Like our fears, it is worry, insecurity, and uncertainty that exists within our emotions. With all these combined, they create emotional obstacles. These obstacles will cause more stress, the stress then causes us to feel overwhelmed, which also limits our personal growth.

There are so many things that matter in life that it can seem overwhelming. Why? Because we put self-imposed emotional obstacles in front of us – stopping us from experiencing even just the simple things in life. In other words, we create the complicated life we live in. Unfortunately, many of us live our lives full of self-imposed obstacles that seem to prevent us from taking appropriate actions and enjoying a fulfilled life by growing from it.

The most regrettable aspect of these undesirable feelings is that we have now blocked any anticipated actions from reflective experiences in our mind before they even happen. In other words, when we proceed with the necessary physical actions, we worry about the outcome, and many times are then stopped in our tracks. And even when the actions are completed, we worry they won't be successful if we apply them; thus, there is limited or even no attempt to grow at all.

To replace these feelings regarding worry, we must change. We begin by asking questions: Am I worrying for the right reasons? And are these reasons then telling me there is something I need to change before acting upon them? Or is it truly some type of fear: fear of rejection, fear of loss, or fear of failure that we must contend with. Whatever the nature of our fears, we must find courage to face these fears. The key is to not give them power and give them energy to take hold.

Truly and simply, by worrying, insecurity, and having uncertainty are only emotional choices that we are creating. Not to mention, these are also your choices that you are alone making. In other words, they are all self-imposed. You always have a choice to have these feelings, or not. These undesirable feelings come from within regarding the emotional belief that you are powerless, but the truth of the matter, you are never powerless unless you are accepting it.

For many of us, we worry too much regarding our life and the way in which we live it. So much so, we make it complicated. We all do. Begin with asking yourself: How much of my time is spent worrying and not having balance in my life? Many of us worry about things that are not within our control. When we worry too much, we lose touch with life and all the wonderful things life has to offer. Who wants to live their life like that? Time for a change. In other words – stop worrying and start living!

There may be a period of insecurity and uncertainty. You may ask yourself: What should I do? What if you answered – well, nothing. When you do nothing, you become comfortable with uncertainty. The results then leave you with limited possibilities of growth or closed off altogether. This also means uncertainty will be a dominant factor in what you do and prevents you from taking action to initiate change to grow. And the results of this uncertainty? It's basically a lose/lose proposition.

A New Attitude

Unfortunately, those that live in insecurity and uncertainty remain where they are and keep doing whatever they are doing. For them, only the how changes, not the what. In other words, we may understand that we need to change, but do nothing to initiate a change. We all deal with hardships, insecurities, and some uncertainty. It's a fact that dealing with daily adversities is hard for anyone, but if we learn to recognize life's difficulties with a new attitude of creating positive feelings, we can then respond to life with a different set of eyes that look for opportunities. And when we do this, we go beyond our emotional worries, insecurities, and uncertainties to apply the necessary actions to grow in life.

How many of us make life so complicated that we spend most of our time emotionally worried and stressed? With our fast-paced and competitive world, it's easy to feel this way. Unfortunately, feeling worried and stressed will not help us move closer to applying actions to promote personal growth. In fact, I bet you could name people that are close to you that seem to be full of worry, stress, and are irritable most of the time. Why is this when it doesn't have to be? This emotional worry provides no known positive benefits and can weaken your faith, destroy your inner peace, make you feel powerless, and will suppress any actions you are wanting to make to grow from them.

Negative People

Feeling stressed only complicates our world. And when we are stressed, we can also develop a negative attitude. This negative emotional attitude acts as an obstacle that then creates unnecessary issues in our lives. A negative attitude doesn't just happen all the sudden. Because our attitudes are emotional functions, it starts with what and how we think, then turn into feelings. Remember, everything begins with our thoughts. The ability to change what you think is under your direction. Which then we can also change our feelings. And if this is true, we can change our feelings to an attitude of being more positive.

But what happens when we spend most our time with others who are negative and by the way, also have complicated lives? Well, hint here – we are allowing others now to influence us and yes, our own self-induced obstacles can also come from those around us. And why is this? Well, we allow it. Unfortunately, we will at times, allow others close to us to influence us regarding how we live our lives. Yes. Often it is from the people around us that affect us in discouraging ways from making positive changes in our lives to promote growth.

For example, you have the close friend that says something like this: 'And so life is.' 'You know you can't change it.' Are you kidding me? Really? That's only if you want to believe it to be. The beauty is that you can change your feelings regarding your beliefs. Beliefs. They are your beliefs. Yours only. You have complete ownership. So, why would you allow others to affect your own beliefs? And these are the same people we are supposed to trust, respect, and value.

We should all be aware that striving to go beyond our reflections to learning, then growth will, at times, be stepping out of the security of where we're at today. But this stepping out will be challenging at times and we don't need others to discourage us. When others say these discouraging things, we then struggle with our self-confidence. Remember that these kinds of obstacles are self-imposed and only by our choice.

Because others can affect us, we must understand those that oppose us, are not good for us. The decision to live your life is your own responsibility. Your action or inaction becomes your own responsibility. Often other people will have your values and beliefs that are in conflict with yours, and when they see you living in opposition to their values and beliefs it can threaten them because, in a way, it is not their way of life. Be the secure one that lives their life with their own set of important and personal values and beliefs – be you.

As we discovered in this chapter, there is seems to be a tendency of our emotions, or feelings that lead to obstacles to growth. Also remember that all along the way beginning with inner drive thoughts and feelings, then outer drive responsive actions, and even before we apply actions to attain growth, there will be gaps. These gaps are filled with barriers and obstacles we must resolve before moving forward. May it be our beliefs in ourselves, procrastination, fears, worry, insecurities, uncertainties, or even negative people, we all have the power to overcome these self-imposed obstacles and change our emotions to positive energies, making good choices, and applying effective actions to move toward our personal growth.

CHAPTER 11

GROWTH IS A CHOICE

CHOOSING TO ACT

As we learned in the previous chapter, it is our emotions, or feelings that are many times the obstacles in striving for growth after we take our compelling actions. Further, whether it's emotional beliefs, procrastination, worry, fear, or even negative people, it's still our choice not to allow these obstacles to prevent us from our personal growth. And as we discovered, all these emotions listed are indeed self-imposed. Yes. Growth is truly a matter of choice.

So, choices. We choose our choices. In fact, every inner drive thought, every feeling, and every outer drive action is our choice and is also under our direction. Where does this leave us? Well, it's like this: All the reading, reviewing, and even embracing the principles I have shared thus far in this book mean nothing unless you choose to act upon them. Therefore, we need to talk about choices to grow.

It is not what you say, wish, hope, or intend that matters; it is only what you do. Your actions on a minute by minute, hour by hour basis tell you who you really are and what you really want in life. You are who you are, and you are where you are today because of all your previous choices up until this current moment. Think about that for a moment. At this very moment, you are making a choice to read this book. You are also choosing to attempt to embrace the content of this book and a choice to keep reading.

Choices are about right now. Today. We can only change today. Today is what we control; not yesterday and not tomorrow – just today. You cannot change the past, but you can choose to change today, right now. You can accomplish more and exciting things in the future just by making better choices today for growth and striving toward your personal potential for the future.

The only way to grow is with outwardly compelling and committed actions. Remember, it is our outer drive that goes beyond mere reflection from our inner drive functions of thoughts and feelings. Now moving forward, enters our outer drive. Our inner drive provides us the confirmation, energy, and motivation to an outward movement of outer drive actions. Here, with an outer drive, we are choosing committed actions to learn and grow.

This outer drive does not express itself with equal intensity in all people. Some feel a strong urge to build, create, become involved, achieve, and make an immediate impact upon the world. Others, experience a more natural expansion that comes with growing and have blossomed, moving them to an outwardly, and seemingly more assertive actions taken for growth.

Choosing Abundance Over Fullness

Let's discuss more upon our intensity levels. Life is all about choices we make – or not. The choices we make also have consequences attached to them. As it relates to growth and fullness in one's life, it is only a matter of choice to feel this way. In fact, we can choose to go beyond fullness to abundance. Why beyond fullness? Isn't that good enough? Well, first, the idea of good enough will not move you beyond your reflections to choose to take the necessary actions to grow. And secondly, I will tell you that the feeling of fullness is only temporary. Fullness, for many of us, is truly not good enough.

Think of it this way – being completely full after breakfast in the morning, not wanting any additional food during the day. Now that doesn't really satisfy most people. Most of us also want lunch, supper, and snacks in between throughout the day. And don't forget dessert! We should all strive for not just full but wanting abundance in our life. But why abundance?

Another way to look at abundance is linked to personal growth. The opportunity of abundance is the effort of pursuing greater personal growth than you believe you can. Unfortunately, many of us stop right there – just the possibilities, but no further advancement. Remember we talked about beliefs in a previous chapter. Our beliefs, if we allow them to, can be obstacles to our personal growth. Just the belief of being less than average can be an obstacle. So, what stops us from pursuing growth is struggling with feeling less-than. Like all emotions, feeling less-than is only our choice. Why not make a choice for abundance? Abundance unfolds within you – never hold back your abilities in choosing to be more as you accept that abundant growth is not automatic, you must believe in yourself, you must give effort, and most importantly, you must choose it.

This topic of choosing abundance truly matters as it relates to also choosing your growth potential and the use of your abilities. It is those that choose abundance in their abilities that also discover the true richness in life. When you make the choice of abundance you continue to strive for greatness – striving for additional knowledge and skills that promotes personal growth. It is our choices focused upon abundance that results in success after success.

Choices Regarding Our Actions

You have two choices while in reflections regarding potential for your actions – limitations or possibilities of bonding to them. We talked about limitations in Chapter 4 as a barrier. Here, we are comparing limitations to possibilities. One choice restrains us, the other creates endless opportunities. Limitations only impede the possibilities of learning and personal growth during reflections regarding the compelling actions that we are planning to take. But, if you start all reflections with unlimited possibilities, your thoughts would be endless. Endless possibilities create thoughts of abundant actions in your life. The only barrier from thinking and reflecting this way is yourself.

All choices in life start with reflective thoughts of what *could be*. To have a life of endless possibilities begins with what we think of ourselves. To create everlasting opportunities, we must go deep within reflection and have the thoughtful focus of having *no obstacles* that can get in our way in achieving the actions we want to accomplish in life. Endless possibilities suggest thinking and reflecting with abundance and no restrictions in choosing the necessary actions that will lead us to our personal potential.

Consequences of Our Choices

Again, life is, for the most part, filled with many choices. These choices we make create the consequences that are the results of those choices. In other words, we make the choices or decisions that are under our control and direction, but the consequences of those decisions are uncontrolled. We indeed choose our choices.

The choices we make in life affect us in many ways. They can affect us negatively or positively. They can be short or long-term. Making good choices is the understanding that these choices must be made at the right time, with the right attitude, and most importantly – for the right reasons. That also means it is only by choice that you choose to grow.

When choices are made quickly, most times they're considered efficient or doing things right. Doing things right is a good thing, but not always the best way. Wait a minute. What? What if I were to tell you that being efficient isn't always best? Have you ever compared efficiency to effectiveness? What about effectiveness? When you take the time to pause and have a positive attitude – you're being effective or doing the right things. Do you see the difference? Doing things right versus doing the right things. The key? Pausing before taking actions. With pausing, we can think about our choices, and consequences of those choices, to be effective; thus, doing the right things. So, if you think about it, efficiency is really more of a convenience. You are doing something right, but are you doing the right thing? There is a very distinct difference between the two ideas. I would like to think of effectiveness that is linked to success – *always* doing the right thing is *always* the right choice. This is effectiveness.

This also means that you have the power to choose how much growth potential you have. Why is this? It is because you are doing the right thing, not just timesaving for the sake of getting it done. We get to choose how we maximize our growth through always being effective. That, my friends, is the key. We alone, *effectively* choose our choices.

The Choice to Change

I believe most of us want to grow in life. This means not wanting to stay in the same place. It is that intent to grow in life that focuses on the commitment to keep moving forward in life. What we need to understand is that making the choice to grow will also require us to change what we do daily. This change involves changing our behaviors, and at times our environment.

I have always believed that if you don't like something in your life, it's simply a choice to change it. Your growth potential is only possible if you change what you're doing today and what actions you take tomorrow. That kind of growth mentality uses change as a component to reach greater heights toward your personal potential. I also believe that during some point in everybody's lifetime there comes a time that requires us to look at our current life and reflect upon what actions are necessary to change it.

So, let's go back to actions. I believe we can all agree that it is our actions that are required to create change. In response to making the choice to grow, we must indeed also make changes in our life. And as I previously mentioned, these changes affect our daily behaviors.

I also mentioned our environment as a possibility of required change. What's unfortunate about this requirement is that many people seem to have no urgency to change. They're stuck where they are in life with the same minimal patterns of living, truly wanting to be more but are unwilling to sacrifice changing their lives. They stay in the same place and never realize what potential for growth they have within. This is truly unfortunate when they are choosing this lifestyle over what they could have but quit before they get started.

So, what about our environment? In order to grow and strive to reach our growth potential, we must also be in the right environment. For many of us, being in the right environment also means change. You might ask – What is the right environment for growing? The right environment consists of one with less stress and complications. A place where it is conducive for learning and growing to flourish. A space in your life that remains positive and healthy is the perfect environment to promote growth. How will you know you're in a perfect environment to grow? It's about how you feel within. This environment I speak of is less stress and no complications, only calmness and positive in nature.

What about change? So, we just change what we're doing, and we automatically grow? Did you know, it's possible to change without growing. Think about it. We can change the way we do certain things and still not grow. Why is that? Just because you do something different does not automatically turn into growth. One of the keys to making the right changes that will allow us to grow is knowing the difference between a fact or challenge.

What is the difference? Well, challenges we can change, and as for facts, there are some uncontrollable truths of life, which we cannot change. For example, you cannot change how tall you are or how old you are, but you can challenge yourself to change your attitude toward them. That's the difference. Our choice, our approach, or our attitude.

Let's go back to challenges. A challenge is different. A challenge is something you can do something about. Again, it's our response to these challenges, or our attitude of choice that guides us. For example, if you're stuck in traffic, you can change your attitude about the traffic and look at it as an opportunity to listen to your latest audio book or turn off the radio and do some reflective meditation, or just listen to your favorite radio music station. Believe me, no one likes to be stuck in traffic. The key here is although it's a challenging situation, we still have choices as to how we respond. Challenges are just that. They can be thought of as tests.

Testing Our Choices

We discussed tests previously regarding our barriers and obstacles. Tests in life. Those that understand that tests are a big part of our life are also the ones that regard life as a training ground in which we are continually being tested. And because our life is a series of choices, we are also tested upon those choices. Basically, asking us the question:

Did we make the right choices? But why are we continually tested? It is because this testing is meant for hard work on our behalf to make this life training worth all the efforts for our personal growth. There is a sense in which the realization of this testing is just one of the multitudes of not just hard and humbling work, but also liberating us to understand this testing is all meant for us to grow. Yes. These are growth tests. These tests are there to build you up. To make you stronger. To help you grow.

If I were to ask you – 'Do you want to reach for increased growth that moves you toward your personal potential?' I believe most of us would say yes. But that's the problem. Again, most of us have intentions to grow, but many of us don't choose good choices to pursue growth.

And why don't we create good choices to pursue growth? I think it's because of our individual situations in life. Why is this? Because it is our situations in life that are mainly based upon the choices and the actions we have made – or in this case, failed to choose. If we go back to the right environment for growth, this then would be a perfect example regarding why we are limited in promoting our growth. Why? Because we feel as though it is the situations in our environment, our overall living conditions, that they make us feel as though they are keeping us down and we can't get back up to face them. This of course is only self-imposed obstacles that we are choosing.

So, if you are stuck where you are today with limited growth, it is because of the choices you made yesterday. If this is true, it's time to change those choices. Sounds easy, but much more difficult to implement into our lives. It's truly unfortunate that we tend to put obstacles in the way. We can accept or defend that changes are necessary, or we can cover it up. All three options require choices. But understand you're going nowhere until you change your choices.

Whether you want to accept or defend the reasons why there is no or limited growth in your life, you have the ability to change it. As for covering up why you refuse to grow, then you must ask yourself: Are you attempting to hide something? Is it someone on the outside that is holding you down? A difficult environment? Or, is it just who you are?

Whatever excuses you used to answer those questions, understand this – that it is never too late to change. You need to reflect upon the actions you're taking today and think of what you're truly capable of doing. Our current situations in life are mainly due to our choices. Life is a series of choices, then actions. Make the right choices, complete the right actions.

Taking Responsibility for Our Growth

We talked about responsibility previously in the preceding chapters regarding combating barriers and obstacles. In this case, we go deeper into why personal responsibility is important to maximize our potential regarding our growth. Doesn't it make sense that if we want to improve our personal growth, we must then choose responsibility to create it? How we answer this question varies, but we know in our heart that this is a choice. Choosing responsibility in one's life is ours alone, not someone else's job. Why is this? Because there are many times that we have the tendency to blame someone else or some life situation for where we are in life, our circumstances, and even our choices we have made. We need to overcome that tendency of blaming if we want to increase our potential for continuous growth and live a life with no limits. Think of it this way – If we are willing to make choices that increases our sense of responsibility as it relates to our growth, we will also see a corresponding increase in our successes. Isn't that what we want in life? Many more successes, less failures? I would venture that most of us would choose more successes.

Further, think about a successful person. One of the reasons why successful people are accomplished is that they identify and seize opportunities and take the responsibility for the completion of each of those opportunities. It's called effort. How do we give effort? It's simply a choice to give effort. When we give effort, we control how much. In other words, we are making the best out of the opportunity because, this opportunity may not come around for a long time, or never again. (We talked about opportunities in a previous chapter.) Now, most have heard the phrase – here today, gone tomorrow. Well, it's true! Seize the moment! And seizing this moment? Yes. Another choice. It is when you seize moments that growth is realized. Remember, it is the successful people that choose responsibility for their growth. Without this ongoing effort, they could not have increased their continued growth potential.

These same successful people take back control of their own destiny. The only way to take control of the direction of your life is by choosing to take responsibility for yourself and your daily actions. People who identify and embrace their growth are those that are successful in life. Let's go back to the idea of control. Ask yourself – Can I control everything in my life? The answer is – no. Things happen around us; things happen to us. Whether it is around us or to us, these are from the outside and we can't always control them.

The only things we can control is what happens within us that we alone can choose how to respond to them. That's why it's so important to reflect upon our experiences from the inside, out. In other words, our control or directives begin within our reflective inner drive functions to our outer drive committed actions. With this control, we can then choose the actions we want to take according to these experiences on the outside. So, within we reflect, and on the outside, we choose the necessary actions to learn and grow from those experiences. Further, we choose what to control, when to control, and where to control any experience simply from within us. Once we begin taking charge and making our own choices, our life begins to change.

What happens when we don't choose responsibility? One thing is that we suffer from self-esteem problems. In other words, we blame someone, or something for the bad things that happen to us. Remember, we can't always control what happens to us. When this occurs, many of us adopt the victim mentality. This my friends, never leads to growth, it only leads us to failure, stress, and complications in life.

But as we change our thoughts and attitudes to choose what to control when faced with difficulty, we can then move forward regardless of any anxieties we may feel. The results? Great, right? It gives us a powerful inner sense of satisfaction that although difficult, we still faced the difficulty and succeeded. That in itself is personal growth.

For some, it might mean that this growth stuff has made us a self-starter of some sorts. That's a great way to begin. Why? Because many times, it's the self-starter who does not wait around, they just choose to act. And when we realize that we may make a few mistakes along the way, we will choose responsibility for them, and we know that this is also the greatest opportunity to promote our growth.

The Choice of Discipline

We talked about being disciplined earlier in a previous chapter as we must be disciplined to believe in ourselves. As it correlates to choices to grow, we need to go deeper into our discipline regarding our choice to follow-through with necessary actions. If we go back to the subject of responsibility and successful people, we also learn that these same people are highly disciplined regarding their actions. They choose to be self-disciplined. They don't need to be told to act, they guide and encourage themselves within to choose the actions they ought to do, not just the actions they want to do. Why? Because they do the right thing, not the popular thing. Remember, being effective is always doing the right things. And that's what it takes to go from being average to accomplishing effective actions in striving for our personal potential.

Another way to understand this type of attitude is that success is not just handed to us. We don't choose successful actions on accident. That is why it's so important to take the time to use our inner drive strengths to effectively reflect upon every experience before acting upon them.

Before we reach this kind of discipline, we must make the choice to act. But, before this choice to act, many of us get stuck. This is where excuses come in, such as: I will start next month, I will choose to take the action when I feel more energy, and I will act when I am not as busy. I could go all day with the choices regarding excuses not to act.

Want to know a secret? It's choosing actions before you feel like it. Yes! Sometimes that's what it takes. Making excuses never moves you forward. For example, I can tell you as a writer, I have experienced, and still at times, experience those moments when I don't feel like writing, researching, or editing my work. Where does that get me? Same place I left off yesterday and not accomplishing what I want to complete – the next book.

For me, I must have a plan of follow-through even if I come up with these self-imposed excuses. Self-discipline is the fuel that keeps my fire lit. The willingness to keep moving forward even if my inner drive thoughts and feelings are somewhere else. And you say, this works? Yes. It's the pushing through these self-imposed barriers that makes you forget the excuses altogether! It's the power to make the right choices to endure, to learn, to grow.

My plan has always been a self-talk each morning. This has been a discipline of mine for many years. I don't complete my day with complete satisfaction until I have accomplished what I set out to do. And because this works, the promises I keep to myself, I respect myself that much more as I put my head on the pillow at night for a restful, peaceful sleep.

The Choice of Actions Create Risks

I would be remiss not to discuss the importance of our choices while taking actions to grow and how these actions are affected by the possible risks involved. As we reflect upon any experience that requires action, we must also consider the risks implicated for each action taken. The choice of taking actions will always involve risk, and at times, more than others. All the self-esteem and self-confidence doesn't mean avoiding risks. But don't get me wrong, these strong emotional values are sure helpful when you're taking risks. The bottom line is to move forward in life, and it will involve risk. It will also be your choice as to the level of risk you are willing to endure according to the actions implemented toward your growth potential.

I believe most of us would ask ourselves questions that relate to the possible risks before choosing actions according to the reflective experiences we have. Remember we discussed the importance of pausing and thinking through our options before choosing actions. This process is being effective. For effectiveness, what questions would you ask of yourself? Personally, I would ask questions like, 'What is the worst thing that could happen?', 'Will it improve my chances for success?', 'Is there room for error?', or once I have reflected upon my risks, I would ask: 'Do I believe it's the best action to take?' Note that each question involves choice. The more questions you ask and answer, the better prepared you are to weigh in on the risk and gauge whether the risk is smart or foolish. In other words, by asking these questions, you determine if the risk is worth the efforts, or if taking the risk will undoubtedly fail. Smart or foolish, you choose.

Overall, risk is rarely comfortable for anyone. Even a smart risk can makes us feel anxiety. Why? Because it requires us to get out of our comfort zone. Even being out of our zone is risky. Look at risks regarding dealing with your emotions and doubts. If you remember, we discussed how our emotions can be obstacles to our personal growth efforts. I believe one of the biggest issues is the possible losses involved. Most of us look at losses as failures. But in reality, losses are really just a great learning and growing opportunity. Remember, it's our approach, or response that makes the difference. Think positive. Often times, losses can create learning lessons that are carried throughout life that provide us with valuable personal growth. You must move forward with actions making yourself continually comfortable being uncomfortable. Yikes! Read that sentence again. Well, doesn't this feeling of being uncomfortable also create insecurity and uncertainty? We talked about how fear can cause us to feel insecurity and uncertainty in the previous chapter. Being uncomfortable is similar. These feelings get us out of our norm, and therefore these feelings create more emotions like insecurity and uncertainty as well.

What to do? We must challenge ourselves to change what we think. Instead of the negative feeling of being insecure, uncertain, or uncomfortable, think the opposites – secure, certain, and comfortable. It's truly only a state of mind. You simply change what you think. This is where a positive inner drive comes in. And when you change what you think, you change how you feel. When you can be successful with being calm regarding the feeling of uncomfortable, you can win the day! Let's go back to the idea of losses. One strategy to use is instead of avoiding losses, learn from them. You would be kidding yourself if you thought that all the actions you choose will be successful. There will be losses and many more wins, but you must choose to take the risks. Regardless of the outcome regarding the risks – success or failure – you ask yourself one question. This question is: What did I learn? When you seek lessons more than you avoid losses, you become more comfortable with risk. This is exactly what I mean by being comfortable being uncomfortable. Bingo! And you also grow personally from these losses.

So, what do you think is best for taking risks? It's going to require some personal courage. If you want to expand your growth, which includes improving your overall life, you need to be willing to take whatever risks are necessary to succeed. You will need to do this on your own. You will need to gather the courage to do what others may not do and not for the sake of choosing actions that are considered bold and risky because you think you can, but because you know that these actions will provide personal growth. These actions are what I refer to as smart risks. They are worth the effort and sacrifices. You have heard that there are *costs* in life. These smart risks are worth every *penny*.

The wonderful thing about taking smart risks is that they not only expand your reflective possibilities, but you continue to grow. So, are you willing to increase your risk choices? Are you willing to fail as a result of taking some of your actions? Are you willing to learn from those failures? Are you willing to move away from your comfort zone? These are tough questions, but worth saying 'yes' to.

Your Choice for Growth

It is our outer drive that must activate itself to push us beyond mere reflections from our inner drive. Now, you understand why I shared the term *inner drive* in Chapter 5. It is our inner drive that is always communicating with our outer drive. It's our call to action. It's our inner drive that prepares us to move forward with the necessary and committed actions regarding our outer drive. In other words, it is our outer drive function that leads to an outward movement into the form of actions.

Now this outward movement in the form of actions is also a choice. It's always a choice of when, how, why, and down the line of reasons for growth. A good example would be the intent to grow regarding higher education. Many people want the four-year degree, but how many will choose to do the demanding work to attain it?

According to a study done in 2019, only 35 percent of Americans have a bachelor's degree and less than 14 percent have a masters. Seems alarming to me, but much truth in it. That being as I am a professional life coach, many of my clients, young and old, choose higher education as a life goal. And don't get me wrong, it's a wonderful goal to improve your knowledge level. The choice is the intention, backed by the committed actions that will result in attaining the goal. Many of my clients are indeed excited by the idea of higher education. But an idea is really only an intention. I find that the biggest obstacles are choosing the efforts, the hard work, the actions to complete the course work is where most fail.

Understanding this, it is those that have this compelling, strong urge within that will be the energy to move them beyond their inner drive, to the outer drive of choosing appropriate actions to learn and grow from. As we grow, we will experience the natural expansion that comes with the growing that has developed within, moving us to an outwardly remarkable, with seemingly more assertive energy, and then pushes us to take the lead to an extremely eventful existence of personal potential. This my friends, is a perfect example of how our inner drive is continuously communicating with our outer drive function. It is by our inner drive of reflection within that directs our outer drive to action. It is this formula of going beyond our reflections to choosing necessary actions that promote personal growth.

But, as I have previously shared, it's ultimately your decision regarding your choice to focus upon how far you can go in life. It's truly about our mindsets. But understand this, a mindset that believes there are limits to growth are those that reach a specified 'limit' and go no further. Now, go back to the example of higher education. Yes, it's a choice, but the focus is upon the actions you must take to grow from the experience is where the effort truly counts. On the other hand, those that have a growth mindset, will always be choosing to move forward, searching for that next learning opportunity to increase their development and choose committed actions to strive toward their personal growth.

Those with this type of mindset are also continually challenged. We talked about challenges earlier. So why repeat? Because a person that is challenged and has the mindset of growth, is also striving for learning from the challenge. When we are challenged, it also means the wonderful opportunity for new discoveries we can make along the way. With new discoveries, comes new knowledge, and this new knowledge brings us growth. This becomes the motivation to realize there is always something new to learn and grow from in life. We also realize that this learning is lifelong There is no *completion date* and there is no asking the question: Are we done? It's more the question of: How far can we go? The answer – the possibilities regarding your choices to grow are endless.

We must make a choice to keep moving forward with our choices to take the necessary actions to keep growing. Yes. We must choose our choices. And if you remember, we just talked about risks. We know that there is no possibility of growth in our comfort zones. It's all about taking smart risks to push beyond our comfort zone of merely reflecting within, and the continued efforts of striving forward regarding our growth zone of appropriate actions on the outside that makes the true difference.

We also talked about failures. Growth and failure go together. If you fail, you can learn and grow. Failure is inevitable; learning and growth are the options, or choices. Both growth and failure are considered consequences of our choices.

In many instances, there is a need for changes in our life if we want to grow. Changes are choices as well. We must change our behaviors and our environments if we are to grow. And this change is not without being effective, or doing the right things. In addition, creating changes in our life to grow also requires us to take responsibility of these changes. Further, as we make the choice for taking responsibility, we are also creating self-discipline. It will be this self-discipline that will keep us on the right track for personal growth.

Lastly, we must desire opportunity and make the choice for growth. There will be many doors of opportunity on your path. You must open and walk through those doors in order to go to the next level in life. As you choose to open each door, there will be risks involved. Remember to be comfortable being uncomfortable. There will be 'good' and 'bad' doors, but you must open all of them. At that time, you have the choice to keep the door open or to close it. These are merely chapters in our life. There will be many chapters – one begins, another ends. We must strive to keep turning the pages of our 'book of life'. There are many more chapters in your life, start living them by choosing continuous learning and growing along the way.

But if you do need to close a door, learn the lesson first before closing – then move on to the next, and the next, and the next door. Understand, opening or closing these doors are simply choices you are making. The more doors you choose to open, the more growth you attain. The results? You will change and you will continuously grow. All opportunities are focused for your growth. Don't miss a one.

By choosing to grow, you are fully aware of your ability to improve. If you continue to develop these abilities, you are already making the choice to grow. There are no limits. You can do more. It's only by choice.

CHAPTER 12

STEPS TO GROWTH

OUR INNER AND OUTER DRIVE'S INTERACT

In our last chapter, we discussed how growth was not automatic and that we must make the choice for our personal growth. But once we make a choice to grow, there needs to be a process, or steps that leads us to that growth. As in most processes regarding life improvement, we must take the proper steps. In this case, before learning or growth is a realization, we must first go deep within our personal insights which are part of our inner drive. Once we complete the process of our inner drive measures, we can now focus upon our outer drive regarding committed actions.

If you want to grow and become the best person you can be, you must be intentional about it. In fact, just about anyone would agree that growing is a good thing. But why isn't everyone taking the necessary actions to grow? Unfortunately, growth is effort and requires us to change. Why unfortunate? Because it's a fact that many people are reluctant to change their current lives to grow. In fact, we touched on the topic of change in the previous chapter. For any efforts of learning and growth, change is required.

Here's another fact: If we don't change, we don't grow. And if we don't grow, we are not living up to our potential in life. Why? Because growth requires us to surrender our current state and take the necessary actions that will make us leave our comfort zone. Secondly, we are all meant to live up to our personal potential. We must first understand that growth is a choice, a decision that can have a dramatic difference to your life. Let's put it another way. Most people don't realize that unsuccessful and successful people do not differ in abilities. They just vary in their desires to take the necessary actions to grow personally or professionally. But it's the successful people that know and understand this very important virtue – if they want to be effective in life, they must keep growing.

The Inner Drive Foundation to Growth

Understanding how to get to this step in the growth process can be an obstacle for some. Being stuck where we are because we choose to be, or it could be that we are just unaware as to where to begin regarding the growth process. Well, it's like this, whether you are stuck or unaware, if you follow the steps explained in this chapter, you will be well on your way to creating your own growth potential.

This chapter is based upon the effective steps to growth. So, we must start with a foundation. The following (7) measures are an integral part of the inner drive foundation to taking the next steps necessary to move you forward requiring outer drive actions that will lead you to your personal growth. We must consider these foundational inner drive measures or guidelines, before we submit and create outer drive actions:

Foundation One: Continuous Improvement

The people who strive for reaching personal potential are those that choose it. We just spent an entire chapter based upon choices for growth. It begs repeating here. If you don't make the choice to grow, there is no growth. It's that simple. To strive for personal potential requires growth. A vital part of that requirement is that you must think in terms of continuous improvement.

On the other hand, if you think by staying where you are today and hoping for success, you are mistaken. The only way to improve the quality of your life is to first improve yourself. So, the bottom line is that if you want to take the success journey, you must live a life of personal growth. And the only way you will grow is if you choose to grow; thus, continuously improve yourself.

Foundation Two: Start Now!

Many of us love to use the excuse of – someday. Remember, we just mentioned the idea of *someday* in the previous chapter regarding barriers and obstacles to grow. The point here is that *someday* is today. Why wait? Growth does not just come to us; we must produce it. We must act. And no matter where you may be starting from, keep moving and don't become discouraged by anything in your way. Think of it this way: for every person to have gotten to where they are, began their journey where you are today. There is no time like right now to get started. Recognize the importance that personal growth plays in your daily successes and commit yourself to continuous development. Today!

Foundation Three: Never be Content

Growth equals wins. Wins like losses are only temporary. That also means that you must keep growing if you expect to be successful. Don't settle into a *comfort zone*, and don't let successes *relax you* as well. Not to say, don't take the time to pause and recognize your successes, just don't celebrate too long. You must keep moving forward to the next growth opportunity. Remember in the previous chapter we discussed our comfort zone. It's easy to be satisfied where you are today and stay there; and many people do just that. But if you want to do more with your life, to continually grow, you must take the appropriate actions to get to where you want to go. The bottom line is we can't stay idle in life if we want to grow.

Foundation Four: Continually Learn

The best way to keep from being content with your current successes is to be continually learning. Note: Learning. It's another avenue of continuous improvement. What does this take? Time and effort. You must plan each day for something new to learn. Now, that's effort!

Foundation Five: There are Trade-offs

A trade-off to grow can cause us stress. Why is this? It is because developing yourself can be uncomfortable. In other words, to focus upon developing yourself, be comfortable with being uncomfortable. Growth requires time, effort, and discipline. This also means less time for leisure activities. Just remember, the payoff for this trade-off is continued growth that leads us to our personal potential.

But wait. Is all this trade-off stuff really worth the extra time and effort? Well, look at it this way: growth is always worth the trade-offs because, let's face it, the alternative is limited growth with unfulfilled potential. Again, your choice. We all know we can do better. Success regarding increased growth takes time and effort and you can't make the journey if you're just sitting back waiting for your life to improve without effort.

Foundation Six: Questions Before Actions

To produce better outcomes, thoughts of asking yourself a series of questions are essential for positive results. These questions must be answered before moving into actions. While reflecting upon an experience, we must consider what actions to take. In this considering phase, our thoughts go from asking ourselves the question: 'What can I learn from this experience?' *To then asking:* 'What is the possibility of growth that I can apply from this experience?' *Then lastly, more assertively, you ask*: 'What actions will I take to grow from this reflective experience?'

Note that these three questions leave nothing to chance. By using the expressions of 'What can I ...' and 'What is the possibility...', and finally, 'What actions will I take ...' all represent affirming and action-oriented phrases that will result in creating effective and positive outcomes. Positive outcomes are only possible by fully *experiencing the experience*. It is through *experiencing the experience*, or action-oriented responses, that true growth begins.

Now that you have affirmed the necessary actions to be taken, it is now time to be accountable, or to own your intended actions. When you own something, it motivates you to get results. By owning your outcomes, you are investing in your individual growth. The more accountability and responsibility you invest in yourself, the closer you move to personal potential.

Foundation Seven: Going Deeper with Personal Insights

This is our final measure in the foundational process. We now go beyond merely reflecting upon our experiences and move these reflections into our personal insights. This insight is your inner drive initiating your call to action. This is the final measure as you begin the process of outer drive actions leading to growth.

Going deeper into reflection turns each experience into personal insight. It is personal insights that prompt us to take effective actions we need to initiate. And when we act, it moves us from simple self-awareness to compelling and committed outer drive actions that help us strive for our personal potential. This same personal insight brings together the previous foundational measures of inner drive thoughts and emotions of continuous improvement, starting, never being content, continually learning, contemplating trade-offs, and asking ourselves questions.

The goal moving forward is to release the powerful inner drive thoughts and feelings of our reflections and attaching them to actions to reach personal potential. This process starts by unlocking our thoughts and feelings of our inner drive to strive for our best in life. Personal potential is your own individual best efforts to being more than you have already become – making your best better. It's personal because it's about you and your passion to fulfilling your true potential – a purposeful achievement to enrich your life.

The Six Steps to Outer Drive Actions

So, we have discussed our foundational inner drive measures to move us closer to our outer drive of actions. Let's now initiate how our inner drive measures interact with our outer drive efforts that will contain the necessary actions to create growth.

The (6) steps of moving from inner drive responses to action-oriented steps to growth are important to understand, embrace, and initiate daily. These (6) steps move us from simple responses regarding our reflections to taking compelling and dynamic actions, thus learning, and growing from them. Our last foundational measure of personal insight begins with a personal commitment to initiate these six effective actions daily. Let's begin our outer drive of actions by making an appointment with yourself ...

Action Step #1 - Make an Appointment – with Yourself

Each morning set aside time to make an appointment with yourself to reflect upon your daily experiences that require actions to be taken. By intentionally making this appointment, it is completed as an outer drive action. Start with the previous days' experiences both successes and mistakes. The successes, you want to continue to repeat each day.

The mistakes are for improved self-awareness to embrace learning to be applied from your reflections.

It's unfortunate that most people fear mistakes more than they want to learn by them, but when you learn from your difficult experiences, you can apply encouraging actions leading to your personal potential.

This appointment with yourself may involve past experiences. Yes. You may also reflect upon any past events where added learning could be initiated. It is never too late for learning to take place from past experiences. With learning comes actions to apply toward self-improvement areas to enhance your life. When reflecting, we choose from present day to past experiences.

Action Step #2 - Think – Drafting the Action-Plan

Remember that everything begins with a thought. Although still an inner drive function, it is now moving from thoughts, then to paper which is an outer drive action. Before acting, you need to think about an action-plan. Part of this process begins with personal insight, but we now take this process further by putting the action-plan together. In other words, drafting the plan. Strong thinking starts within and deciding what you need and want to change as you create your plan of action. It is at this time that we ensure we have completely understood all the previous foundational measures. It's that extra effort to ensure we are being effective and taking the right actions. Again, it is effective actions that must be initiated to strive for growth.

Now your thoughts move to creating responses as to what needs to change. These changes are initiated from the first action of reflecting upon your previous days' events or something from the past.

As we get closer to responses, actions flood our minds. It is when our minds are flooded that we must, at the least, take written notes.

Hence, our draft plan of action begins to take shape. These actions many times are from new perspectives regarding our personal insights. The newly discovered reflective perspectives will prompt us to respond in some way. It is these responses that lead to unproven actions we will need to take. This outer drive response of written notes then becomes the draft to our action-plan.

We must be aware of unproven actions that can also cause undue pressures. Remember, this is only a draft which also means there is room to adjust if necessary. Rather than hiding from these pressures, rise above them. As a result, you don't let pressure define you. When you release any pressure that you may feel, it then provides you with an open mind and heart to create better outcomes from your reflective experiences.

Action Step #3 - Talking to Yourself

After thinking and writing out a draft of our plan for action, it's talking to ourselves that becomes a natural occurrence. Again, like the previous action step, although an inner drive of talking to yourself, it is this process that is considered communicating to your outer drive for taking action. Now, our inner and outer drive's interact, as both functions are needed to complete the process of reflecting, then responding to provide learning and growing, and finally striving for our personal potential. When you reflect, you are talking to yourself. These are the most important conversations you can have to create outer drive actions to your inner drive reflections. Self-talk has potential to have great impacts on us. In these self-conversations, we can choose to stay positive even if it's a negative experience you are reflecting upon.

Further, reminding yourself that these reflections are for better self-awareness to apply beneficial learning from your mistakes. This valuable learning while reflecting gets you closer to becoming the person that you were created to be through the actions you will take.

Action Step #4 - From Talking to Writing

As you have now completed all your previous measures in making an appointment with yourself, inspired your thoughts, and initiated self-talk; it's time to move into writing down your ultimate plan. In this case, we are going beyond our draft from Action Step #2 to the creation of our final plan.

When you take this time to write, you are making the final directive to your outer drive as committed actions are beginning to take shape. This step might be the most important – from our foundational process to our action steps of now pen and paper. It is when we see our writing on paper that it seems to jump off the page and be recognized for the importance it represents. This is your final plan before committed actions take shape.

The inner drive of thoughts and feelings from your reflective experiences must be recorded as an outer drive action as so you don't forget them. You will not have a clear direction unless you can state your committed actions in writing.

Further, writing makes you think things through. When you then write down your intentions, again you will want to answer a series of questions before moving onto potential actions. In other words, it forces you to think about and record all your options and perspectives before moving forward with demonstrated physical outer drive actions.

Action Step #5 - Develop Goals for Your Plan of Action

Once you have in mind what you want through your written plan, you now need goals regarding the plan. Goal setting is simply making choices. Goals are not just promises to ourselves, they act as commitments. They are also not dreams; they are committed actions to be taken. So, it's going from what you want to where you want to go, thus the plan. Your success is determined by your goals regarding the plan of action. Again, these goals should be in writing. Your written goals will give you a guideline to follow that will help eliminate unforeseen obstacles, distractions, and interruptions. It will also serve as a written tool to show progress as you complete each task regarding your plan.

Yet another advantage of written plans are that they reinforce your goal commitments to attain what you want. It will continue to act as a reminder of your plan's objectives and the reasons for following them. Lastly, your goals regarding the plan of action will continually let you know where you have been, where you are, where you are going, and any adjustments that may be required along the way.

Action Step #6: Apply with Actions

This is the most important step. The previous five steps lead you to this one: committed actions. Now having the knowledge from the previous chapters, you must put all this valuable information to work. Growth is realized by the committed physical actions we take that lead us to results. You must now apply what you have learned from your reflective experience through taking the necessary outer drive actions.

Asking Questions Toward Growth - Follow-up

Now, we have discussed the term follow-up previously in Chapter 7 – Time for Action. As this was an inner drive function, here in this chapter we are measuring how much growth occurred regarding our completed actions. In fact, for effectiveness in anything you do, follow-up should always be a vital part of any process completed.

We're not done yet! Now that you have the foundation of the roles of both inner and outer drive's, we can look at the entire process and focus on a follow-up process. Remember being effective is doing the right things. There is no complete process without a follow-up. This growth follow-up consists of asking yourself questions. In other words, you took all the necessary steps to get this far, and even the right actions. Now for better self-awareness and enhanced growth, we have follow-up questions.

Let's go back to the questions asked previously in Foundation Six: Questions Before Actions: 'What can I learn from this experience?' *To then asking:* 'What is the possibility of growth that I can apply from this experience?' *Then lastly, more assertively, you ask*: 'What actions will I take to grow from this reflective experience?'

In asking follow-up questions regarding your growth potential, we now focus upon the next questions in the growing process. *The first question should be*: 'Did the completed actions lead you to growth?' If you can't answer this question, is there a barrier you have not thought of? Whenever I am thinking and reflecting and feel like there's a barrier, I need to ask myself more questions. For example, if I am trying to learn something new or delve deeper regarding an action I took so that I could grow, I will ask myself follow-up questions. You should be spending a lot of your life asking yourself questions. When you ask questions, it's to challenge yourself. *The questions would include*: 'Did I take the right action?' 'Could I improve on that action?' N*ow, ask again*: 'Did I grow as much as expected from that action?' *And if you answered 'no', ask another one*: 'What could I have done differently to experience a better outcome?'

I cannot overemphasize how important it is to ask yourself challenging questions as it relates to personal growth. And if you ask the right questions, they will lead you to the right answers. In other words, if your questions are focused, they will stimulate creative reflective experiences that have occurred that match the actions you have taken. Why is this? Because the results are new possibilities and insights into future actions that you can take. If these questions are from the heart, are honest and direct, they will lead you to solid convictions regarding your outer drive actions. It's sort of planning your next steps for future outer drive actions.

Follow-Up Questions Regarding Well-Being

Let's go deeper. We discussed how the follow-up process works for our completed actions, what about your overall well-being as it relates to self-improvements for growth to occur? I believe the first question might be: 'Do I feel successful in life?' If you answered 'no' – ask – 'why'? The answer will help you know where you are in life and what you need to do to change your answer regarding your success level and what improvements you may need to include to grow. Note: Even if you answered 'yes' to your success, there is always room for improvement in life. Again, remember our foundations to growth earlier in the chapter. Success doesn't mean you have reached your personal potential of life; it just means you can go further. As I mentioned earlier, the truth is, we should never feel as though we have reached our pinnacle of potential but striving for it through our committed actions should always be our outer drive focus in life.

Writing Out Our Follow-up Questions with Answers

It comes down to what you want to accomplish in life and where you are on your journey will then determine what actions you need to reflect upon regarding any experience you have. The most important thing you must do is to write out these questions. In Action Step #4: From Talking to Writing, was our outer drive regarding a written plan for our actions. Here we are writing our follow-up after the completed actions have taken place. This outer drive action represents writing down your questions, as they are for you to see and embrace. These questions will assist you in developing your self-awareness. Now, start writing answers to the questions. They may not come right away, or be complete, but write! Why? Because we discover that what we reflect upon is now written on a page. It might even be different than what we thought. This writing will help us discover answers we need to know before acting upon them while striving for growth.

Let's be honest. All of this sounds like a lot of effort. You're right; it is. Unfortunately, that's why many people don't follow-through with it. But I will also tell you, that all this effort is worth it. Reflect upon this – the farther you go in life, the more important it is to take the right actions. Right actions lead to learning and growing. Never forget that your goal in personal growth is striving to reach your personal potential. (We will talk a lot about our potential in the later chapters.) Here's the good news – if you're willing to make the choices to put in the time and effort to grow along the way, you will also be successful in life.

This book is to inspire you to go beyond reflecting through your inner drive of thoughts, feelings, and most importantly – complete committed actions of your outer drive to grow. And throughout this process are choices all along the way. After reading this chapter, you are now aware that you have the tools to take the next steps to necessary outer drive actions and further enhance and enrich your life. But to enhance and enrich your life you must choose to be determined and have dedication. In other words, if your inner drive reflective thoughts can conceive it, your outer drive actions can achieve it. Yes, indeed, our inner and outer drive's do interact.

It's taking the time and effort to flow through the foundational steps as well as the six action steps. But it doesn't stop there. We must perform a follow-up by asking ourselves important questions for maximum learning and growth potential.

The only way to achieve your desires and dreams is to act upon them. The greater you trust in yourself, your beliefs, and your thoughts, the more actions you will take. Now take the necessary time to put your actions to work to move you closer to growth fulfillment and personal potential.

What we could do changes as we develop. What we should do also evolves. But think about this – could and should – really gets us nowhere. It's when we initiate the dedicated steps to act that growth is realized. By going through the foundational and action steps, we will find success.

What we must do is leave behind some old things and take on new ones. The process of adaption and expansion never stops. These steps to growth can be challenging work, leaving our comfort zones and making mistakes to expand, but if we are willing, our lives will positively change.

CHAPTER 13

SELF-IMPROVEMENT LEADS TO GROWTH

In the previous chapter, we discussed one of the foundations to growth was continuous improvement. In this chapter, we will go deeper into what, why, and how our efforts of self-improvement will lead to growth. Let me just start by saying no matter how good you have become; you can become better. Note here I mention *become.* As you read this chapter, self-improvement leads to growth which also means that both improvement and growth are continuous efforts throughout your life. In fact, self-improvement and growth are almost synonymous. By self-improving, you grow. When you grow, you are in fact, self-improving.

So, this next comment may surprise many, but here goes. No matter what you have accomplished in life, you will never reach your *full* potential. We discussed this idea early in the book, but it's something we must understand if we are to self-improve to grow. It's difficult for some of us to hear but read on. I want you to think in these terms: Reaching for our potential is a pursuit without an end. You don't have a finish line, you keep running – improving and growing all along the way on your journey called life. This is exactly why I termed this journey as striving to reach our personal potential. It's personal to just us. We are all unique as to how much potential we have within and how much we are willing to strive for it.

So, growth? Is it something we should expect more from ourselves? Is it the thoughts of once we finish school, we don't need to learn anymore? If your goal is to grow, these questions must be answered with a firm sense of there is much more work to do in life. Then, there are those that have the sense as though they are done with the idea of self-improving. Thinking and feeling this way can be even more difficult to comprehend if we believe we want to grow in life. Being done with something does not link to personal growth.

What is the result of low expectations regarding improving our life or knowing we have the degree; we are good, right? The belief here is that we have already reached *good enough growth*, and if we push ourselves to the next level, we may be disappointed. Why? Because with this mindset, we would expect more out of ourselves. What this means is, if we did not live up to those standards, we would then be disappointed in ourselves. So, to avoid this feeling of disheartenment, we then lower our expectations.

Well, if you believe you have discovered the disappointment of not going to the next level in life, you will never choose to improve and to grow. To self-improve and grow, you must be willing to risk all the previous disappointments, the experiences attached to them, learn by them, and then discover – well, you are not near as bad as you thought. Further, we now have the experiences of these difficulties behind us which also means we have the opportunity to embrace the learning from them. And the results? A wonderful way to provide us a self-improvement foundation to grow upon.

All-Knowing Can Delay Your Growth

Let's go one step further. How about this notion? Not just that we believe there is no longer a need to grow, but we go beyond thinking we already know it all. Remember, we discussed the idea of too much belief in ourselves in Chapter 10. This notion is similar. It is when we go to the next level of believing we know it all, we feel as though it is no longer necessary for growth. Yes. There are times we can go beyond the idea of self-improvement to the belief we know more than we think we know.

It's true that we all have a certain level of ego. Some egos are over-the-top, others so low they don't have much confidence in themselves and have low self-esteem. Being confident of who you are is a good thing but being egotistical is going too far. The problem exists when a person with an all-knowing attitude feels as though they have no room for self-improvement.

As we reflected earlier regarding ourselves personally, what if we concluded that we are overall too confident? If we indeed discover that we do feel this way, it could be an obstacle to our self-improvement efforts. We all know people who believe that there is nothing more to learn in life. They know it all. If you have that kind of attitude toward enhancing your life, you will never reach your personal potential. In fact, show me a person who thinks they have all the answers, and I will show you someone who is most likely failing in at least one part of their life. This is the type of person who believes they are all-knowing, and no other person can teach them anything more than they believe they already possess. This type of person also does not realize how much they are depriving themselves of continuous enhanced knowledge and skills to self-improve their life.

This unwillingness to listen and learn from others is only going to hurt their personal potential of reaching their highest levels of success in life. In their reflections, they have already reached the pinnacle of life. Their ego is bigger than they are. Unfortunately, their reflections and mind-set are already closed to the rewards and enrichment of continuous learning and growth. In truth, none of us will ever reach being perfect.

And why is this? It's because life is a continuous path of discovery, and we must always be self-aware of this most important path and stay on it. Learning opportunities are all around us. It is called life's lessons when we reflect upon any situation or event resulting in learning something new about ourselves. These should be times of excitement regarding the opportunities to discover new things in life. By discovering new ideas and perspectives as you reflect upon your life, you will see the world with a different set of eyes. When we experience these exciting new ideas and perspectives regarding our life, it is the same time that we begin to realize our self-improvement possibilities.

Learning is a life-time event – we can never be all-knowing. The key is to open our mind and open our heart while reflecting upon our lives. This allows us to focus upon embracing new ideas, knowledge, and skills. Reflective experiences upon self-improvements lead us to take different paths – discovering new and exciting adventures with continuously learning along the way. Always stay hungry for knowledge. Never stop learning, never stop growing toward your personal potential in life.

Self-Improvement Through Our Mistakes

One of the major areas of self-improvement is created through our mistakes in life. Note that we mentioned mistakes in the previous chapter as well. Also remember that there are gaps in between all inner, as well as outer drive functions. This is all part of the journey. Mistakes are made all throughout the self-improvement process. But also remember, mistakes provide us great opportunities for learning. Learning from our mistakes is created by taking actions to correct them. It is when we go beyond reflecting that we learn from our mistakes and take appropriate actions to not repeat these same patterns of mistakes. Well, we hope.

We can simply choose to continue to produce the same mistakes or make choices to embrace the learning that reflection allows us to experience. When we reflect deeply upon mistakes that occurred from the past, we can also develop steps to learn from them.

In the real world, life is not always surrounded by successes. The truth is, life also includes our mistakes, or how I like to think of them as *learning opportunities*. The wonderful outcome of reflective experiences is that they help us to improve our self-awareness as well as learning more about ourselves to make better decisions that help us move forward in life.

Self-improving through our mistakes is wonderful, but it means little if we don't know how to turn the lessons into benefits. It is the learning and lesson application regarding reflection that are the foundation to experiencing the benefits from our mishaps.

Pausing and thinking about what we could have done differently to change the actions of our past to successes are the benefits you are searching for when reflecting upon them. In truth, mistakes are just opportunities for learning something new about ourselves to self-improve and enhance our lives.

Embracing Learning from Our Past

Let's discuss the idea of past mistakes a bit more. The past is filled with many opportunities to learn. When we learn, we improve ourselves to grow from our reflective experiences. We just discussed self-improving through the experiences of our mistakes, but why stop there? Don't just focus on daily mistakes, but all experiences. Even those from the past.

Reflection regarding our past experiences is the key to better understanding ourselves. Unfortunately, many of us don't take the valuable time to pause and reflect each day. The consequences of not taking this beneficial time to reflect, results in limiting the uncovering of our past and therefore less opportunity to learn by those experiences and the valuable lessons that lie within them. It is from these past experiences that we can continue to create more self-awareness and take actions to improve our lives.

It is by choice that we initiate reflection regarding our lives. Whether it be current day or from the past; they both provide us opportunities to improve ourselves. If we realize the importance of truly embracing who we are and experiencing reflections each day, we then can move closer to self-improving and growing in life.

The Power of Questions Regarding Improving

If you're looking to improve your life, you must start by asking yourself questions. These profound questions must be asked without fear. This is a time to be completely open with yourself. With freedom from any self-imposed fears that you may have had in asking yourself deep, personal questions, you can now release the power of questions that will create the answers you are searching for in your life that will lessen any fears you may have.

Now, wait a minute. Why would you focus upon questions when what you really crave are the answers? It's quite simple. Answers come from questions, and the quality of the answer is directly determined by the quality of the question. So, ask the wrong question, get the wrong answer.

Then it makes sense to ask the right question, get the right answer. Not exactly. There are many ways to ask the right question, but most of the time, we ask easy, quick fix questions to get to an effortless, right answer. This of course is ineffective. Think bigger. Ask the most powerful question possible, and your answer can be life altering.

So, what kind of questions should you ask yourself as they relate to self-improvement? Let's look at our careers for example. How about asking: 'Have I learned all that I can regarding my current position?' or 'Have I learned all that I can regarding my leadership qualities?' or how about 'Have I learned all I can regarding my health benefits?' and 'Have I learned all I can regarding my departmental goals?' I could go all day here. The point I am making is that we can always learn more about anything in life by asking powerful questions.

Reflect Upon You

After asking the right questions regarding life events, situations, and experiences, you must focus upon yourself. It will be reflection that will provide us the best conduit in identifying areas of improvement. When you get right down to it, there are occasions when we have a little pressure reflecting upon ourselves and how we live our lives. Why? Because we open ourselves up to possible flaws we may have.

Previously we discussed asking questions without fear. Same in this case. When you reflect upon yourself, always believe in your abilities and move beyond any fears you may have. Discovering our flaws, and doing something about them, is how we self-improve and grow to move forward from being average to the best we can be.

When we reflect upon ourselves, it's easy to try to hide our feelings. When we attempt to bury our feelings, the only person we are fooling is ourselves. Do you find yourself hiding on the inside, afraid to be criticized by others for who you are? Unfortunately, we hold back due to feelings of being an outsider – Why? It may be because we feel as though we are singled-out by others due to our uniqueness.

We should all embrace this thought, for we are all unique. Understanding our uniqueness is a wonderful thing. Being unique is what separates us from everyone else. Embracing who we are during reflection is vital to defining the actions we will take to self-improve and grow in life.

What's Your True Character?

What does our character have to do with self-improvement and growth? How we appear to others reflects who we are – our character. We just discussed our uniqueness. Therefore, others see us for who we are and will judge us. Our character is observed by the actions produced and the things we voice. Many of us hold back as to who we truly are because we are afraid of being singled out, criticized, ridiculed, or embarrassed. You can see how this would affect our self-improvement and growth efforts.

A good example of this feeling is holding back our individuality. This occurs many times in relationships with others as we are trying to be someone else while in the relationship. Have you ever reflected upon a relationship whereas you were not being yourself, but who the other person in your relationship wanted you to be? The bigger question might be: Are we self-improving for ourselves, or are we doing it to satisfy the wants of another? We have all been in situations where we try to make another person happy at the expense of being who we truly are. This expense comes at a price. It is our self-esteem that is affected by what we think, reflect, and feel about ourselves. If we allow others to dictate who we are, we lose our identity. We need to be *who we are* regardless of what other people think – do not be worried about acceptance by others, just be happy being you.

If you have any doubts, you need to ask yourself: 'What is holding me back from being who I really am?' Is the person we see in the mirror one that wants the most in life, to self-improve, to grow in life? Unfortunately, some of us hide or limit our character as not to appear as *different* to those around us. When in fact, we should all be proud to reflect upon who we are within as well as how we demonstrate it on the outside.

Where to start? The best place to start is embracing who you are. People always project on the outside how they feel on the inside. Character is about how the person feels internally and that overflows into how he or she acts. In other words, if we are positive on the inside, it shows through our actions on the outside. Be who you are and express it on the outside. Being more self-aware will only improve our life.

Knowing 'Why' We Want to Self-Improve

Once we can identify who we are, we must dig deeper into knowing what and how to improve ourselves for growth. Once we reflect upon what and how, the most important thought is *why* do we want to improve? What and how will take us only so far. It is only by asking ourselves *why* we have purpose, and purpose requires action. The *why* will keep you motivated. In addition, a strong *why* will help you keep going when the actions become more difficult, tedious, and at times, discouraging. If your self-improvement is attached to purpose, you will understand *why* you're taking actions.

It will be natural that your *why's* will expand. When they expand, you will put that much more effort into the actions you take. The bottom line is if you're connected to your purpose, you will be more successful in your efforts regarding self-improvement.

Self-Improvement is Self-Validation

Now understanding *why* we need to improve; we must next validate ourselves. One of the most helpful benefits of focusing upon our reflective experiences is that they make us feel validated while self-improving. In other words, our life experiences create a feeling that we make a difference and mean something to this world. Regarding self-improvement, feeling validated will help us move more confidently forward in life.

Is it only through self-validation that we should feel valued? The answer to this question may vary. Validation regarding ourselves and the life we lead signifies we are somebody. Think of self-validation as a way of feeling you have confidence, passion, and purpose. It's saying to yourself – I'm worth the efforts to improve. If you don't have these qualities, it will not lead to self-improvement. Everyone wants to be somebody. It's a feeling of importance; that we matter. It is when we are valued by others that our self-esteem increases. This type of reflective validation provides self-confidence and a belief in ourselves that helps us want to improve and moves us toward our personal potential.

Helping Others Feel Validated

Let's go one step further. Our own validation can also be used to assist others regarding their individuality. When we feel validated, we can influence others as well, so don't stop with just yourself being validated. Everyone wants to be validated – to be valued and highly regarded by those around them. We discussed being valued in a previous chapter. Being validated means you matter. That's all. When we extend this type of reflective thinking and actions toward others, it then helps them feel validated. In addition, they will also see themselves as someone of importance. Imagine how much of this positive energy will now create a tremendous opportunity for you, and others, to grow in life.

The fact is, everyone wants to be somebody whether they verbalize it or not. Being somebody is also being validated of our own pure existence. Why not help others feel like they matter too? If indeed this is something we all have a need for, then we too, can assist others to feel important as well. If other people feel validated, they not only focus on themselves but reach out to provide the same validation to others. As we reflect, why not make it an expectation of ourselves to help others feel validated as well? Further, knowing we need others for our own success, our growth potential will be that much more impactful.

Sacrifices for Self-Improvement

Reflection upon certain sacrifices we have made in life will humble us. In fact, it is these sacrifices that got us where we are today. Sacrifices also come to mind as we focus upon our self-improvements. Sacrifices come in many forms such as – time and effort. We can use the previous example as we help others in their validation efforts. These acts are sacrifices to you in the forms of time and efforts. But, as we discovered, these sacrifices help with our own self-improvement and growth efforts. Yes. These efforts and more of these types of sacrifices will create the improvements we are striving for in life.

When we reflect upon our lives, there are always sacrifices we make to go from one level to another in life. These sacrifices come in the fashion of priorities, or what needs to be completed, and when. A person that is organized also understands priorities. Occasionally, urgent matters come up that get in the way of the important things; hence, important matters are sacrificed for lesser, more urgent ones.

So then, the question remains regarding the priority – is it important or urgent? More reflective questions now start to enter your mind: If I were to actually put extra efforts in accomplishing goals, are there not then other things I will have to give up or put on hold? This is a great question with an honest answer of – yes. When you reflect upon anyone you know that has achieved self-improvement and growth in life, you will also realize that this person made many sacrifices to do so.

The willingness to sacrifice is to give something up. The choice is made depending on the importance of the sacrifice in question. In life, sometimes giving something up may bring success later. Effective people know they need to sacrifice in their life and to dedicate themselves to become the best they can become.

As it relates to importance, we need to make two lists as we reflect upon this subject: 1) the things we are willing to give up accomplishing a goal, and 2) the things we are not willing to sacrifice. In all honesty, sacrificing usually means being willing to temporarily give something up or trade something of value you possess to gain something more valuable that you currently do not have. Remember, we discussed trade-offs in the previous chapter. Same goes here. To self-improve and grow can create sacrifices. Sacrifices can also be hard choices to make.

There are many sacrifices as they relate to self-improvements. Time and effort are just two of them. As we reflect upon what actions we need to take to enhance our lives, sacrifices will come into focus more clearly.

Limiting Your Abilities Will Affect Self-Improvements

We have discussed our character and being self-validated. We have also mentioned limiting ourselves regarding barriers and obstacles in our learning efforts. Here, we talk about how limiting ourselves affects our personal growth attempts. Without having strong character and self-esteem, we will possibly limit our own abilities. By limiting ourselves only acts as a barrier to growth. Remember that self-improvement leads to growth. When we reflect upon limiting ourselves in anything we do, we are only hurting our self-esteem. It is when we limit ourselves that self-improvement becomes difficult to accomplish. To self-improve, one must have confidence in themselves that they are up for any task at hand.

There are occasions during reflecting that we stop short of what we think we can accomplish. This hesitance regarding our thinking process and knowing that we can do more, is limiting our abilities. Selling ourselves short is only limiting our greater potential. And limiting ourselves only results in a less than average potential regarding personal growth. Many times, deep within, we all want more in life. Unfortunately, there are those that seem to be happy with just being average and never reaching their personal potential in life.

That's fine for some, but I believe that many of us would enjoy continuously self-improving and growing throughout our lives. It all starts by what we reflect upon – the belief we have in ourselves. Our true potential lies not in limiting ourselves but attempting to flourish to higher levels than we thought possible.

In truth, we all have abilities deep within that go unnoticed unless we tap into them with complete confidence. Why not live life with passion and enthusiasm with no limits attached? There is no limit to what we want or who we can be in life. Again, the only true limits are those we alone create and place upon ourselves.

We discussed limiting ourselves. And like the previous chapters, remember we have also discussed both barriers and obstacles. To self-improve for growth, we must face these difficulties again. Because in striving for personal potential, we must fill the gaps of barriers and obstacles with positive, compelling, and committed actions. Sometimes it's only a matter of thinking differently.

It's Only a Matter of What We Think

If we think differently while reflecting upon our abilities, the opportunities are endless. Imagine life in terms of no limitations placed upon us. Would we live life differently? I believe most of us would live our lives another way. What if I told you all you must do is to think differently? When we go into deep thought and reflect upon having limitless abilities, we can experience the endless possibilities that will improve our lives.

Life is not about limiting ourselves; it is about continuous growth. To grow, we need to reflect upon and know our strengths and possess the will power to take risks; otherwise, we cannot set a direction to follow on our life's journey of self-improvements leading us to personal growth. When it comes right down to it, growing in life has no limitations – the possibilities are truly endless.

Also, we must remember that every reflective experience begins with a thought. If you want to improve yourself, your thoughts will lead you to what things you want and need regarding enhancing your life. Thoughts are only the beginning of the inner drive process. To create self-improvement opportunities in your life, you must take appropriate outer drive actions. As we reflect upon how to improve ourselves, we can suppress our feelings about them, or we can take the necessary actions to become the best we can be.

It all comes down to choices. The choices we make are ours alone to follow-through in creating a life-long commitment to improve ourselves. Each day we make choices while reflecting to improve our circumstances or remain the same. Take advantage of each day to learn something new and when you do, you will move closer to your personal potential.

So, when should we start improving? First the obvious answer: Today! Right now. Think of it this way – you need today to be every day. Remember, you will never change your life until you change something you do daily. That also means developing great habits. Discipline is the bridge that brings us closer to accomplishing our goals. This *bridge* if you would, needs to be crossed each day for successful results. Over the course of time, that daily crossing becomes habit. And ultimately, you will no longer be deciding what results you want to experience, they will become your daily habits. If you take the right actions regarding your reflective experiences, you will see the results. Habits that help you reach fulfillment are ones to keep. Look at each day as taking at least one action to create positive habits and you will win the day! These actions will move you to self-improvements that lead you to your personal growth.

As we discovered in this chapter, self-improvement and growth are interchangeable. Both principles move us forward on the path to our personal potential. Whether it is learning from our past mistakes, reflecting upon ourselves and our character, making sacrifices, or understanding limitations, we must focus upon how improving ourselves will lead to personal growth. To grow is to succeed in life. To grow is also a choice. How will you choose?

Or let's look at it this way. Imagine your life differently. A focus upon self-improving daily to grow in life. The only thing you need to do is to think differently. Think about how you can increase your abilities, knowledge, and skills. We all have the tools within. It begins with our inner drive of powerful thoughts and feelings regarding the steps to self-improvements that in turn, motivates our outer drive actions that help us grow.

CHAPTER 14

ACTION POTENTIAL

Potential is different to everyone. Some believe they have reached it to their fullest. As I have mentioned previously in the book, I believe striving for maximum potential is a lifelong journey. Additionally, our full potential is unattainable but moving toward it acts as a challenge and a way of life for those that want the most in life.

Moving is the key. Think in these terms: There is no moving without actions to get you where you want to go. It is our action potential that motivates us each day to be our absolute best in whatever we are doing to reach our personal goals in life.

Action is another word for doing, but what about potential? We have discussed striving for our personal potential throughout this book. But what does potential represent in the context of *action potential*?

Just the word – potential – should suggest another word – possibilities. Potential is one of the most underutilized tools that we all have within us. The fact is, all of us have varying degrees of potential. If this fact is indeed true, then all we must do is choose what level we want to use this powerful growth component of potential within us. As in possibilities, potential is a term that looks forward with optimism. It's filled with hope and faith. In other words, faith is the confidence in what we hope for and is the assurance regarding what we do not yet see. Unseen or not, it's there. It promises success. Potential is a word that implies fulfillment. And with all possibilities available to us, we should all be excited about using this potential.

Let's go back to the word – *action* for a moment. Action and potential don't automatically result in growth. That's not how growth works. Growth is an intentional effort. You must seek it. The only way to seek growth is by taking actions. As this book is about taking actions to grow, it is through seeking our potential within that will lead us there. In other words, to reach for potential, we must take the appropriate actions; thus, *action potential.*

Hard Work Leads to Growth

Can I tell you something? Hard work does not always lead to growth. Wait. What? If we work hard, there should be something we receive, right? Yes, it's absolutely true. But, if you're anything like I am, you will have one or more mistaken beliefs that create a gap between the idea of growing and reaching for your personal potential.

Let me explain further. The mistake many of us make regarding growth, is thinking that by simply taking actions of hard work that we will automatically grow. Yes, mistakenly, we have all had the idea that just because we work hard at something, we grow. But that's not how growth functions. By just working hard doesn't mean you will grow from those extra efforts. In fact, it will hold you back from being as intentional as you need to be.

We are deceived by thinking just hard work will help us reach our potential. What's wrong with this thinking? Well, it's like this, just because we work hard at something doesn't mean we don't make errors along the way. These errors stop us from going to the next level on our potential journey. So, these errors stand in the way of progress. It will now take corrective actions to get us back on track. And that is why just hard work is not enough to bring us to our potential. In other words, it's not automatic. To become intentional with our actions to grow, we must expect to make errors along the way. Yes. Hard work sometimes finds errors in our actions. By making these errors, if we take actions to correct them; thus, we grow, and reach for our potential.

Okay, now think about all those previous errors you have made on this journey called life. Those errors that you reflected upon and learned something from, have also promoted personal growth. In fact, there are some errors you are still learning from; thus, more actions are required. This process means we are always learning, always growing, and always striving for our personal potential.

What kind of errors am I referring to? Some of our biggest errors are in our thinking: *I don't need to grow, I'm already happy where I am*, or *I'm too old to grow, I don't have time for growing*, or how about – *I know it all, no growth needed*. We have discussed these self-imposed barriers and obstacles in previous chapters, but in this critical point of striving for our personal potential, we must take the proper, committed actions to move beyond these barriers. If you're one that believes any of these statements, you unfortunately will never take the necessary actions to reach your personal potential.

Inspiration to Grow

Just like having the belief of it only takes hard work to equate to growth, we are all filled with other misconceptions regarding taking actions to reach our personal potential. Another popular one is thinking you need to *feel inspired* to learn and grow. There is no doubt that you know what it takes to learn something new. What should come to mind is that it takes time and effort to have the things you want in life; thus, anything new. When someone tells me, they don't have the time to learn, I tell them that's really all you have – is time. Remember, we just discussed sacrifices of time and effort in the previous chapter.

There are trade-offs to grow in life. Further, I have always had the belief that if you want something bad enough, you will find the time and effort to produce the necessary actions to get it.

If you back that time and effort up with inspiration, you now are motivated with the energy to take actions to grow. The key here is in the actions. Again, all the inspiration in the world is only effective with actions behind the inspiration. Remember, it's called *action potential* for a reason. If you're having difficulty finding inspiration to take actions, please trust me when I say the reasons to keep growing far outweigh the reasons you believe it's not worth all the effort. So, when you think about time and effort regarding the actions you need to take and the growing opportunities to reach your personal potential, just approach it differently. (We will tackle that in a moment.)

Discovering that growth and learning are lifelong also means that the possibilities are endless. The best we can hope for in life is to make the best out of whatever time we have been given. We do exactly that by investing in ourselves and making ourselves the best we can be. Remember, our potential is within and the more we have to work with, the greater the potential and the further we will go in life. Give actions your best and you will become your best. So, how do we start?

We Start with Knowing our Strengths and Weaknesses

If you want to take actions to grow, you must know your strengths and weaknesses. The key for me was to discover my strengths, but just understand that I also have some weaknesses. Why do we need to know about our weaknesses? Because our weaknesses will always be weaknesses. We can get better at them, but seldom make them strengths. So, when I thought about my own weaknesses, I needed to better understand them, manage through them, and make some self-improvements. And that's all. Now my strengths, that's a different story. Discovering my strengths came from a passion within. Matching this passion with my purpose has brought success, peace, joy, and happiness into my life.

This discovery takes time and is unique for everyone. In other words, you must be able to gauge not only where you've been, but where you are currently. How do we do this? It's reflecting upon it. Every action to grow, begins with reflecting regarding the experience you want to act upon. Okay, back to gauging. If we don't gauge ourselves, we cannot set a course to where we want to go. In this case, it's taking actions to reach our potential. Every time we want to learn something new, we must be able to act upon this new thing we've learned today, build upon what we've learned from yesterday, and keep growing to strive for our personal potential.

Unfortunately, many people don't know what actions they could take. Thus, they don't know themselves as well as they should and remain unfocused regarding their growth. Must we know who we are to grow toward our potential? Here's the key – you don't have to know who you are to grow to your potential. What? Look at it this way, you may not truly know who you are, but you do have to grow in order to know what you're made of. So, what to do?

Explore yourself as you explore growth – they go together. It's the same avenue I took. Remember I mentioned passions? You begin by paying attention to your passions. That awareness is necessary as you take actions to grow.

Removing Obstacles with Unlimited Potential

Reflecting and responding with inner drive thoughts of unlimited potential and ability creates a belief that there is always knowledge that can be gained and will show successful results. The fact remains, learning has no limits. Again, the only limits are those we place on ourselves. Further, just when we think we have experienced everything we need to know in life, we discover there is more to learn. Learning is indeed a continuous journey in life.

So, what's the secret? If we have already changed our thinking, what are we missing? It's all about attitude. A person with an unlimited *thinking attitude* is one who lives life with no limitations. So, dig deeper. We are combining thoughts and emotions. There are great and powerful results from this combination.

We all have certain abilities regarding individual skills and knowledge levels – all which can be enhanced. Not just by higher learning, but through life's experiences. Again, learning has no limits. Like many things in life, we have a choice as to how much effort we put into life's lessons. The choice is ours alone. Do not place limitations on what you control. The life we live has no limitations. We create the life we want; after all, the choice is ours to make. Be compelled to choose to continuously learn, to be hungry for personal growth, and you will go well beyond your reflective experiences for overwhelming results.

Action Steps to Take Regarding Potential

Actions. Without them, we remain where we are today. By taking the time to reflect upon our experiences, we are now ready for appropriate actions.

To move you from what you reflect upon to taking actions in striving for your personal potential, begin with these three steps:

Step 1. You must have awareness. Spend time really thinking about where these actions will take you. If it's not where you thought it would guide you, then occupy your time to write out what steps you need to take regarding where you desire to go and re-adjust what you want from these actions. Awareness keeps you focused.

213

Step 2. You must acquire accountability. Few things prompt a person to follow through with their actions like having accountability. And who must you be accountable to? You are being accountable to you.

Step 3. As you are the director of your life, you must act. Yes! One of the steps is – action. You cannot complete the reflective experience without taking action to grow from it. And yes, from action to growth to then striving for your personal potential.

Daily Habits and Disciplines

Our *action potential* depends upon our daily habits. It's these daily habits that we accomplish that in turn make the difference on our path to growth. Okay. Actions. Remember that having the right intentions is a great start, but it is only through dedicated actions that growth is possible. So, it is this *action potential* that makes the difference. It will be the effectiveness of your actions taken that will result in the success that you need for the potential you seek in life.

Let's go back to the idea of daily habits. Want more than just habits? Then it will be disciplines that will bring stronger results. I learned many years ago that if I wanted to experience more success in life, I needed disciplines in place. One of the most important disciplines is patience. Our growth potential takes time. This journey is lifelong, so enjoy the ride. Set daily goals to grow. Be a continuous learner.

Yes. One of the best things you can do for yourself is to be a continuous learner. When you cultivate this effort, you will also gain the value and enjoyment of the growing process. It will be your focused actions that get you there. With action-oriented efforts of daily learning, you will develop habits; thus, disciplines. These habits and disciplines are powerful. In fact, these habits and disciplines are really the actions you take. Now think about all those daily habits. They were all completed by committed actions. All these small actions you take today will lead you to bigger actions that will move you closer to your personal potential.

Our Abilities

One of the most powerful *action potentials* is to understand and use our abilities. We discussed how limiting our abilities can also limit our learning and growth potential. You know you can do more – right? Have you ever thought about your life and realized that it could be more enhanced than it is today? How about more satisfying? If you answered 'yes' to these questions, then you're like many people that think about making their lives better. Why not push a bit further toward your personal potential? The key is to act by using your abilities. Most people only use a fraction of their abilities and rarely strive to reach a higher potential. Why is this? It is because there is no pressure to grow in their lives, in fact, many of us have no desire to go further than we are today. Too many people are willing to settle for just an average life with limited learning, nor growth.

When you hear the word – mediocrity – are you really okay with that? I bet not. Why settle for the status quo when you know you have the abilities to be much more than that? Many that think this way then reflect upon why their lives are not as successful and then realize they have not taken the right paths. It is at that time they then recognize that they could have done more but didn't want to push themselves to be better. How unfortunate. People like this have already identified life can be better, but they don't do anything to improve it.

Want a better life? Then you will have to take committed actions to move from mediocrity to using your abilities to move you closer to your personal potential. You must be willing to leave behind what feels familiar, safe, and secure. You must also give up excuses and push forward with effective actions no matter the self-imposed barriers. You must be willing to stretch your own abilities to keep moving forward in life. What does this mean? It's our ability to use effective actions to reach our personal potential.

After reading this chapter regarding action potential, we discovered that we start with knowing our strengths and understanding that we have weaknesses. Also moving away from self-imposed excuses and not taking actions can stop us in our focus to grow. In addition, using habits and disciplines can help us stay on track regarding our actions that are necessary to grow. Then, finally, using our abilities to their fullest will create our best opportunities for action potential efforts to link to our personal growth.

CHAPTER 15

ACTIONS AND YOUR PERSONAL POTENTIAL

As we have discussed in all the chapters leading up to this one, the journey of striving for our personal potential is filled with steps we must follow to get to this point. We learned, first we must reflect upon our experiences, think about them, create feelings surrounding them, and use our emotions of the heart. These are all considered inner drive functions. After our inner drive functions are complete, we then move to outer drive functions of taking committed actions to learn and grow from the reflective experiences that have occurred whether in the past or are current day experiences. And, oh, by the way, there are gaps all along our journey called barriers and obstacles. All of this ensues before we reach any level of personal potential.

Now this can seem exhausting for those that don't want to do the work to be successful in life. Yes. There are those that are content where they are in life, and that is certainly okay – for them. And then there are those that want to be more successful. If you're seeking more success in life, you must travel further to achieve that realization. Another way to look at it is that successful people are those who are continuously taking actions to move forward in life. Successful people are trying to reach full potential, knowing they can't possibly reach it, but it's all about the challenge and enjoyment of the journey, and not the destination.

These same successful people don't know what the future will hold, but they are willing to act to keep moving forward anyway. Again, it's a challenge to them that is well worth the time and efforts. All they know is that they are committed to a path, and they will do whatever it takes to get to the next level, leading them to the next level, and the next, higher and higher to reach the pinnacle of potential. That is their individual personal potential.

A warning comes with this practice. The more actions, the more successful you are, the more mistakes you will make. But as we have already discovered, it is the mistakes in life that we learn and grow from the most.

Or do you want to be on the other side, those who don't do anything and don't make mistakes. Rather than committing themselves to any necessary actions that may cause alarm for some mistakes along the way, they instead allow themselves to be stagnant in life. They think that if they don't do anything, they are safe. It's really just a dream for them to be successful in which they believe that success is impossible to reach. A dream is a dream. Some are too high, others too low but dreams just the same. Our dreams are what we strive for. Why not take actions to accomplish them? A dream is just an intention until such time you act upon it. We need to take an action, any action even if it ends up being the inexact decision. Whatever we do, it will be far better than not doing anything at all or just waiting for something to happen.

What's the key here? It is taking action. Taking action to reach your personal potential is the foundation to success in life. It's that simple. We want to train ourselves to continually take necessary actions to move closer to our potential. There's only one way that you're going to find out for sure what's right for you and that is by taking appropriate and committed actions. You can think about what you want, you can describe it to yourself, you can gather facts, and you can even ponder the possibilities all you want, but you will never truly know until you take the necessary actions and experience the positive results of striving for your personal potential.

After reading the various chapters in this book; hopefully you have discovered that it is purposeful reflective experiences that allow us to expand upon a deeper sense of introspection of our inner drive. It is this deeper sense that shapes our thoughts, inspires, and stretches our feelings. This process then initiates our outer drive actions to promote better self-awareness that feeds our personal growth. If this improved self-awareness is then embraced and applied to learning, that leads us to personal growth which in turn produces enrichment in our lives.

It is through our effective responses that begin the true connection to our reflections. When we effectively create our own powerful actions, we then begin to increase both mental and spiritual introspection for overall self-improvement and personal growth.

Turning Actions into Personal Potential

This book focuses on our purposeful inner drive thoughts and feelings; immediately followed by outer drive actions. Having intentional thoughts and feelings while reflecting is only the start of the self-awareness process. It is the effective actions you take after your reflective experiences that valuable learning and growth begin to take shape. It is these actions that will lead you to your own personal potential.

It begins with asking ourselves the following questions. Wait. Why these questions? Because it is these two important questions that lead us to striving for our highest personal potential.

1. What is the learning and growth that I can apply after actions I have taken regarding my reflective experiences?

2. What additional actions will I initiate after growth has begun to produce the biggest impacts regarding my personal potential?

First learning, then growth is applied to move us closer to our personal potential and fulfillment. If you are like most, the responses to reflective experiences will seem almost automatic, or natural. Learning starts with responding. And it is responding that is the foundation to growth. Why? Because responding requires us to act. But be aware that responding is only the foundation of the reflective experience. For successful results, purposeful and committed tangible actions must be taken.

After Reflecting, It's Time for Actions

In reflecting, many people do not recognize the value that once they have reflected upon thoughts and feelings of their experiences, they must go beyond reflection to not only simply respond but create effective actions. Not recognizing this wonderful opportunity and potential for personal growth is unfortunate.

Another way to think about it is that although many of us have reflected upon life experiences, and maybe even recognizing some of the potential benefits, we don't go any further to realize the true lessons within these experiences. This, of course, resulting in no follow-through with committed actions to grow from the reflective experiences; thus, no movement toward personal potential.

The true value of reflective experiences is to take actions after you have deeply thought about the potential learning that come from past and current day experiences. With learning comes self-improvement; thus, increasing your growth to strive toward personal potential.

When purposefully reflecting, you must understand that every thought and feeling has the possibility to go to the next level of beyond and can be applied with purposeful actions that promotes growth in a way that personal potential can be maximized.

The Eight-Step Process for Taking Actions

If we are to strive for our personal potential, we must also have steps to move toward it. The only way to move toward something is to act. Taking actions regarding these processes will be the key to your success. Here are eight steps that will provide successful results to help you strive for your own personal potential. In fact, some of these very same steps have been mentioned in some form or another in previous chapters leading up to these steps. They bear repeating here for successful outer drive actions.

This eight-step process focuses upon the guidelines regarding establishing and accomplishing the actions you set out to complete. These steps are powerful, proven, and practical.

1. Decide exactly what you want. Be specific. Don't make the mistake of saying things like, 'I want to be rich because of my actions' or 'I want to be happier because of my actions.' These are not actions. These are wishes or dreams. An action is something clear, specific, and purposeful.

2. Write your actions. Only 3 percent of people have written action goals with clear plans to accomplish them. When you write your actions, you make yourself accountable to them. They are yours alone to complete.

3. Set a deadline for the actions. Determine a specific time for when you wish to achieve the actions. If there are several actions involved, set sub-deadlines for each action.

4. Make a list. Like Step 2, write. This process is like a self-brainstorming activity. Write down everything you can think of that can possibly be done to achieve your actions and keep adding to that list until the list is complete. These are the objectives for each action you want to take.

5. Organize your list. Now, create a checklist of the things you need to complete, and in the specific order that they need to be done. What action you need to do first? Second? Third? If required, go back into reflection. This action will assist you and ensure you are on-target according to your list. Now this list of activities is organized and ready for the actions you have recorded.

6. Now, take the actions according to your plan. Do something. Do anything. But take actions immediately. In addition, create urgency, be curious and consistent while taking these actions. (So important, that we will discuss all three of these areas in more detail next.) Taking that first step is usually most difficult. (Remember your barriers and obstacles.) But the hardest job, are the actions you SHOULD have taken. These are MUST DO actions.

7. Do something every day according to the list that you have created. Do something seven days a week, thirty days a month, 365 days a year. (I think you get the point!) Never let a day go by without taking at least one action regarding your reflective experiences.

8. Follow-up. Daily, have a follow-up session with yourself regarding the results of the actions you have taken. Ask yourself: 'How did I do?' and 'Do I need adjusting?' Adjust as necessary but keep focused upon your actions. This is great reflective time. It's healthy, it's energizing.

Developing a Sense of Urgency

All the steps in world won't get you anywhere unless you develop a sense urgency to take all the necessary actions regarding your reflective experiences. Even with the eight-step process we just previously mentioned, you can still choose to not act. What to do? You must develop a sense of urgency as we discussed in Step 6. If you don't develop this sense of urgency, you could miss opportunities to change your life. We all truly need to understand that the actions we take regarding our reflective experiences will have a long-lasting impact upon our lives.

Look at these previous eight steps as opportunities. If you don't acknowledge, anticipate these opportunities, recognize the impacts, and seize the actions, you will miss the things that really matter. The things that matter are the things you want in life. The only way to secure these things is to immediately act upon them. And after you act, what matters next is the growth you will experience in striving for your personal potential. And that is making a significant difference in your life.

Have you ever had a reflective experience to take some kind of action that you knew would have made a significant difference in your life, but you let it slip away because you lacked the urgency to take that action? I must admit, that's happened too many times in my own life. I wish I could have seized every opportunity that came my way. I know that's unrealistic, but imagine if the desire, the urgency was there, wouldn't you have also done life differently?

In our stressful and busy lives, is there ever a convenient moment to always make a difference? Most likely not. Then, is there ever really the right time? The right place? Not really, but if you lived with urgency, each opportunity would be an overwhelming yes. It's now, right here to act, now! We must embrace and maintain a sense of urgency for seizing the necessary actions according to our reflective experiences to make a positive difference in our life. There is no time like the present. We have discussed being in the present previously in the book. Now is the right time to take the actions needed to positively change our life. Think of it this way: Tomorrow is not guaranteed. Yesterday is too late. Living with purpose means always going beyond reflecting to taking actions to grow toward your personal potential.

Curiosity for Effective Actions

Curiosity can change your life. We mentioned this previously in Step 6 of the Eight-Step Process for Taking Action. Why? Because curiosity will keep you motivated to learn more, hence, grow more. I believe curiosity is the key to be a lifelong learner, and if you want to keep growing, you must keep learning. Curious people are interested in life, people, ideas, experiences, and events, and they live in a constant state of wanting and needing to know and do more.

In fact, it is curiosity that is the primary catalyst for self-motivated learning. People who remain curious don't need to be encouraged to ask questions – they just do it. They already know that the path to discovery is just as exciting as the discoveries themselves, because there are wonderful things to be learned along the way. In fact, it is curiosity that is the foundation to keep you focused upon striving for personal potential.

It is also curiosity that helps us think and expand the possibilities to go beyond reflecting to keep learning and growing. Where does this lead us? It leads to discovery. It also opens the door for new opportunities. Sounds great, right? It's unfortunate that not everyone views life like this. They want to grow but they don't open the door for opportunities.

It's unfortunate that many people fail to reach their personal potential. But here's the key, it's not because they lack the capacity, but they are just unwilling to expand their minds, their beliefs, to break new ground. There is good news – you can change what you think, and as a result change your life. All we have to do is think – curiously. The single greatest difference between a curious, growing person and those who aren't is the belief that you can continuously learn, grow, and change throughout life. The bottom line is that you must be curious to strive for growth and personal potential. It is when we are curious that we gain more knowledge, understanding, and wisdom. But remember this: Knowledge, understanding, and wisdom will not seek you out, you must find them. Being open and curious about learning leads you to growth.

Yet another way to remain curious is to begin each day with a determination to learn something new or experience something different. See each day as an opportunity to learn and you will grow toward your potential daily.

Further, curious, growing people, train themselves to see failure as a sign of progress rather than a sign of weakness. They know that it is impossible to continually try without sometimes failing. It's all a part of the curiosity journey. Therefore, they make failure a friend. What? Failure a friend? The best way to learn is by failing. Remember in the previous chapter we discussed how mistakes provide us with valuable learning for growth. Same in this case. Yes, indeed, failure is the avenue to personal growth. Those that practice this idea will ask questions like: 'Why did this happen?' to 'What can I learn?' and 'How can I grow from this?' As a result of answering these questions, you fail fast, learn fast, and get to try again fast. This mindset leads to growth and future success. The key: Be curious my friends.

Let's go deeper into curiosity. Something that is linked to being curious is never being satisfied. That is, we are always searching for avenues of personal growth. We discussed the idea of contentment in an earlier chapter. What about being satisfied? Let's first ask this question: Are you completely satisfied with your life? How you rate your overall satisfaction is an attitude you choose. After all, satisfaction is an attitude. How unfortunate is the day for anyone when they believe they are absolutely satisfied with the life they are living, the knowledge they have gained, the achievements they have performed, or the opportunities they created for themselves.

This kind of attitude will only attach limits to their progress in life. Yes, a regrettable day indeed that these same most satisfied people never will have the desire to do anything greater that requires seeking further than what they previously believed possible only to pause short of what they were meant and intended to do in life.

The key is to never *be* satisfied. *Being* is responding. Always strive for something – anything. Having passion for your purpose in life will motivate you to continue moving forward regardless of any barriers or obstacles that present themselves. Again, to never be satisfied is an attitude. This means that we get to decide upon whether or not we are satisfied with our life. It's amazing what we can accomplish in life with a mindset of never being comfortable where we are in life. The fact is, we can always improve. We can always strive to be our absolute best and we can do anything we set out to do.

When most of us are starting out in life, we have little to give up and are highly motivated to learn and grow. But as we become more successful and accumulate some good things in life, the sacrifices are at a higher demand of our time and efforts. Thus, we become more comfortable and are less inclined to change because; well, we don't have to.

One of the many dangers of success is that it can make a person unwilling to continue to learn and grow. In fact, many of us are convinced that we know all we need to know, and discontinue our growth, thus remaining stagnant in life. So much so, we begin to think that there is nothing else to learn. No matter how successful you have been to this point in your life, you should never remain where you are today. And how do you do this? It's by staying curious and never being completely satisfied with the potential for growth all around you.

Consistency of Actions

Okay, being curious gets us started on our journey of taking actions, but it is consistency that keeps us effective as we take those actions. We have discussed the importance of being effective with our outer drive actions. The only way to ensure effectiveness with every action is to be consistent. If we are consistent in all we do and find success, we will then experience continuous success in all things we do. Consistency is the key.

Unfortunately, many of us have a challenging time being consistent in anything. Consistency isn't easy, but to be successful regarding taking actions to grow, we must learn to be consistent. If you can believe in yourself, the actions you take, the potential that is within you, there is no telling how far you will grow. You just need to consistently put in the efforts to keep moving forward.

Capacity for Growth

What about capacity for growth? We have learned that our capacity is limitless if we use it. *If* is the problem. The only way to increase our capacity for growth is to stop thinking – *Can I?* and start thinking *How can I?* The difference between the two is the first question challenges you with the idea of whether you can do something. The problem with this question of *Can I?* is that it's filled with hesitation and doubt, that in turn, imposes limitations. The phrase *Can I?* refers to taking risks. When we change the phrase to *How can I?* there is no question, no hesitance attached, and we take the risk with confidence that we will succeed somehow. If *Can I?* is the question you repeatedly ask yourself, you're undermining your efforts before you even begin to take actions to strive for your personal potential.

Further, when you ask yourself, *How can I?* you know you can do something. There is a feeling of unlimited capacity. It assumes there is a way and somehow you will find it. Having these inner drive emotions of self-confidence and self-esteem helps us move toward the outer drive actions for necessary learning and growth.

The most common reason people don't overcome the odds of tangible growth possibilities is that they don't challenge themselves enough. The fact is, they don't test their limits. They don't push their capacity. The greatest challenge you will ever face is that of expanding your mind. The key is that you must be willing to enter uncharted territory, to face the unknown, and to conquer your own self-doubts.

I believe every person has the potential to grow, expand, and be successful. The first step is believing that you can; the second is determination. If you have doubts in your beliefs, you can change your thinking. When you change your thinking to more of a positive belief, you can also believe in your potential. As you get started, it may not look like you're making progress. Don't give in, don't give up on your growth potential. Keep driving, keep moving forward.

Expanding Your Potential

The capacity of our growth is one thing, our potential is another. It works like this: The more growth, the more potential. If you genuinely want to expand your personal potential and therefore your capacity, first change your thinking while you reflect upon your experiences. But a warning, if you change only your thinking and not the right actions, you will fall short of your personal potential.

To start expanding your capacity, stop doing only those things you have done and start doing those additional worthy things you discover you could or should, but most importantly, must do. Doing new things leads to innovation and new discoveries, and among those discoveries is the realization of those things you must do on a consistent basis. Are you getting this? We have discussed curiosity, consistency, and capacity. They all work together to expand your potential. If you do these things, you will continue to grow and expand your personal potential. We must all understand that the process of expanding our potential is ongoing. In fact, it's a lifelong journey. Opportunities will come and go. The standards we must set for ourselves are ours alone. Set your standards high and you will receive high success, set them low and all you will receive is limited, or *locked potential*. Not forwards, not backwards, but remaining in the same place in life.

Daily Actions Creates Intentional Habits

We discussed how important habits and disciplines are as they are linked to our action potential in the previous chapter. In this case, we are going beyond to what I refer to as intentional habits. If you want to improve acting upon your life, it must be in an intentional habit approach. We discussed briefly regarding disciplines and habits that help us stay on track for actions. An intentional habit is done continually with purpose, energy, and passion. Motivation will get you going to initiate actions, but it is only the intentional habit that is developed and practiced where passionate and committed actions can help change your life. Put another way, actions will not change your life in a day, but going beyond reflecting regarding each experience, taking appropriate and committed actions as they unfold, will change your days for life.

Let's go back to habits for a moment. A substantial percentage of what you do, positive or negative, is determined upon your habits. These habits, like positive or negative can be good or bad. Unfortunately, bad habits are easy to form, but many times hard to live with. Good habits on the other hand, are hard to form but easy to live with. Which would you choose? I am going with the good and intentional habits. Doing good and intentional habits will allow success to find you.

The enlightening discovery is that once you develop new, positive, life-enhancing intentional habits, they will soon become automatic and easy. It even becomes harder to revert to a negative habit than to practice a better one because of the feelings of happiness and personal satisfaction that the new habit provides you. And this my friends, is how learning becomes growth, and it is growth that leads to our personal potential.

Now armed with the eight steps to actions, a developed sense of urgency, staying curious and consistent, understanding your capacity, and creating intentional habits for growth, you will have much more success realizing the end results of those actions. The results? Moving you closer to your personal potential.

Our Potential

We all have it. We are born with it. The problem lies with those that don't live up to it. This process is not automatic – it takes time and efforts. Okay, if you have thoughtfully read through the contents of this book, you know that it requires lots of time and efforts concerning your personal potential.

It is only through continuous improvement that we can reach our personal potential. Remember the goal is not for full potential results, it is striving for your own potential, your personal potential. We start with experiences. Life is full of experiences, those from the past and those of current day examples. It is through these reflective experiences that we learn. It is then through this valuable learning, in which growing occurs, that we get closer to our personal potential. It's simple because we all have potential deep within, just waiting for us to apply it. Start today, and never look back.

Let's Get Real

If we don't try to improve ourselves each day, what we have will be the same as everyday – nothing enhanced. We will be stuck in the same place, doing exactly the same things, dreaming the same hopes, but never coming close to our personal potential.

It is what we achieve inwardly that changes our outer reality. In other words, we must first reflect with our inner drive effectively before our outer drive has any success.

Why is this important? Well, first what you focus upon inwardly expands. Secondly, what you focus on shapes how you see yourself and impacts your actions. Lastly, you will never go beyond reflecting until you are *doing* what you need to *do* after your reflection. It's about the *doing* that truly matters in striving for personal potential.

Now is the time for *doing*. There is no remaining still when it comes to taking compelling actions. You are either moving forward or remaining in the same place you were yesterday. Nowhere. Start moving forward today. If you don't, you may look back a year from now and wished that you had started after reading this book. You have gone this far, keep moving forward going beyond reflecting and taking actions toward your personal potential.

Moving forward ...

Taking in account for all the ideas and concepts in this chapter, we can then take the necessary steps to embrace and apply learning from our reflective experiences and take appropriate and committed actions, moving us closer to our own individual personal potential.

The only way to achieve our desires and dreams is to act upon them. The greater we trust in ourselves, our beliefs, and our thoughts, the more actions we will take. Now take the necessary time to put your actions to work to move you closer to fulfillment and personal potential. Do it today!

CONCLUSION

On the surface, this book may seem like a lot of extra effort and work regarding taking committed actions from our reflective experiences to strive for our personal potential. And you would be right, this journey is much effort and work but well worth it. However, if you believe the opposite is true, then I can tell you it is a lot less effort and work to go through life and not taking the actions you really should have or wanted to make. It's only a matter of choice. In my mind, there is only one choice that will improve your life. That choice is to take the necessary actions to strive for personal potential.

Do you understand the consequences of these choices and not taking the compelling and appropriate actions you should have or wanted to make? The consequences result in a less-than personal potential quality of life. You need to ask yourself – is this what you really want in life? To feel less-than regarding your potential when you could have much more significance.

Let's go back to extra effort and work for a moment. Although this book is well-laid out in a logical sequence of learning and growing through actions, it is meant to be easy to understand, and built upon its content and implementation of the material. So, do not be fooled by the simplicity regarding the information I have shared throughout the book. It is truly straightforward by taking the necessary actions in life and following the guidelines stated in this book.

However, this newly gained knowledge isn't powerful until it is applied, and the purpose of this book is not to tell you something new. The purpose of this book is to remind you of what you already know. Believe it or not, you know deep within that it is your committed actions followed-through that amount to learning and growing to inspire you to apply it in reaching for your personal potential. Further, if you applied not just the knowledge, but have a good grasp upon the methods and techniques that I have shared throughout this book, you also know that when you go beyond reflecting to compelling actions for your personal potential, you are fulfilling your life's journey.

Learning and Growing is Through Reviewing

Now that you have read through each chapter, this is a great opportunity to go back and review the chapters – just main titles and sub-titles. As all main titles and sub-titles are in bold to get your attention. Why is this effective? It is when you learn to keep your attention upon all the information, the specific steps, and the examples I have shared throughout, that when put altogether, will encourage you to take appropriate actions from your reflective experiences, learn and grow from them, and move closer to your personal potential in life.

If you exercise the practical methods, techniques, and principles in this book daily, it will allow you to embrace the subject matter and be open to new learning, which allows for more growth. After some time, you will produce positive results that will provide you a new acceptance that striving for your personal potential is a lifelong journey. Remember that what you allow in your life, you also accept. The point is, there are no limitations, only those you put upon yourself.

Question: Aren't you tired of being stressed, frustrated, confused regarding the actions you should be taking according to your reflective experiences? Remember, your circumstances don't change until you take action. As you have now read through the book, are you reminded once again that you *do* have the abilities to create the committed actions you need to take. Remember, you can have anything you want if you are willing to give up any beliefs you can't have the successful life you desire most. Take actions today that will lead you to your personal potential.

Last question ...

How do you plan to use the time that has been given to you?

Remember early on in this book we talked about time. That our time is not unlimited, and we had no control over the time we have, but what time has been given to us.

Ultimately, all we really have is time. It comes down to the manner in which you spend that time. After all said and done, this is the most important time of your life, and if you take the right actions, it can also be the best time of your life. What you thought previously regarding your reflective experiences is now behind you. Now, go beyond reflecting and take the necessary actions that will lead you to your personal potential. For a new opportunity and exciting journey lies before you.

All journeys lead us to paths. We choose our choices. This includes the paths we take in life. Some people are better at this than others. But a lot hangs on to whether we can do it well. Each of us, after all, has been given only one earthly life to live. So, as we each live this one, single life that is ours, we must make all sorts of choices about what paths to follow and not follow. But what makes one path better than the other? The better path is one that is filled with compelling actions that will lead us to our personal potential.

This is not the end, but the beginning of your journey to take the necessary actions that will lead you to your own individual personal potential ...

Best of luck

Gary

ABOUT THE AUTHOR

Gary is the founder of Conflict Coaching Solutions, LLC, a professional life coaching business that focuses on inspiring individuals, couples, and/or groups to transform their conflictive situations into positive solutions.

Before creating his company, Gary was a "corporate coach" for a large utility in Southern California. During his 32 years with this company, Gary designed and developed several coaching courses and workshops that he facilitated to supervisors and managers throughout the company.

Gary has a Bachelor of Science degree in Organizational Management and a Master of Science in Leadership and Management.

Gary also has previously written and published five other books: *The Coach's Chronicles Trilogy, The Reflection Connection – Reflecting and Connecting to Life's Experiences,* and *A Simple Life – Living Less Complicated.* For additional information regarding Gary, his business, or books, go to: conflictcoachingsolutions.com

The Coach's Chronicles
A Journey Through Life's Trials and Triumphs

In writing this book, I am expanding upon the experiences – the connections – of both the trials and triumphs of this journey we call life. What I have found is this connection is only achievable with mindful thoughts, combined with heart-felt emotions. Only then, can we begin to understand what I term as; *emotional connection*, which provides more understanding, passion, and purpose for life's experiences.

The book focuses on seven key areas: *Our Heart, Our Relationships, Our Attitude, Our Time, Our Growth, Life's Lessons*, and *What You Think*.

In this book, I take you through a series of *The Coach's Chronicles* regarding these seven key areas to share each trial and triumph that we all experience daily.

Each Chronicle begins with an INTRODUCTION, or a foundation as to its origin and the thoughts for which have significance to that Chronicles' connection. Then directly after each Chronicle, there is an AFTERTHOUGHT, or a reflective summary behind the true meaning of the experience.

The Coach's Chronicles II
It's Your Story! Start Writing It!

The inspiration that evolved into *The Coaches Chronicles II* originated from a desire to share with others regarding how to interpret the experiences we call life. These are the memorable events and unique life experiences – *emotional connections* – that we proudly share with those relationships close to us. These same memories and life experiences are those that our legacy is built upon.

This book provides the actions and template for each of us to examine and create our own *written chronicles*. We will take the journey together – step by step – through the initial introduction that establishes our approach to exploring the feelings associated with each memory. We then reflect upon the outcomes of each experience in writing our own life's chronicles to share and inspire generation after generation.

The Coach's Chronicles III
Everything Matters

In this third book of *The Coach's Chronicles*, I explore the possibilities of living a life in which *Everything Matters*. The concept and motivation behind this book originated as I was editing my second book; *The Coach's Chronicles II – It's Your Story! Start Writing it!* As I was reviewing the draft of the book, I came upon a chronicle that I had recently written that was titled: *Everything Matters*.

I began to think about how true it is that all we say and do really does matter. Simply defined; *Everything Matters* is an attitude and a profound connection to all things in life.

With a focus of *Everything Matters*, you will look at your life with a different set of eyes in appreciation of *everything* around you. A fulfilled life is one that acknowledges all things as they unfold, then pausing and reflecting upon each event to *experience the experience*. For our life is a series of events, some more important than others, but all experiences are a vital part of *Everything Matters*.

The Reflection Connection
Reflecting and Connecting to Life's Experiences

Do you reflect upon your life? The answer is yes. We all do. But do we all participate in purposeful reflection connections to help create better self-awareness regarding our life's experiences that can promote enrichment in our lives? The answer unfortunately is few of us truly encounter the essential and wonderful stage of effective reflection upon our lives – connecting to them.

In this book, we take a journey into our reflective thoughts, feelings, and responses that guide us to a life-changing introspective regarding how we connect to our reflections. In short, the reflection connections shared in this book are created intentionally to help us embrace our thoughts and express our feelings. These thoughts and feelings then lead us to responding with self-assurance for the foundation of connecting to life's experiences.

A Simple Life
Living Less Complicated

Life, it should be simple – right? The answer is – it can be if we choose it to be. It's unfortunate that many of us struggle with the fact that life really can be simple with less stress and complications.

For the purposes of this book, I choose to include common areas regarding what I believe are required to help create a simple life. Although common, these key areas of our life must be first acknowledged for what they are, then responded to with purposeful actions for their use in striving for a simple life.

I have divided the material into different sections that I believe are all extremely relevant to the 'simple' principles that one must obtain for living a simple life. For they all have a distinct purpose for attaining a simple life.

In this book, I shall present my own personal experiences regarding a simple life that I have focused upon for many years. These experiences, which are drawn from many sources, have contributed greatly to a life that I have firmly established – a simple one.

Beyond Reflecting
Actions Lead to Personal Potential

Are you ready to take the next steps to truly getting something out of what you reflect upon daily? Why reflection? Well, we do more than just think about our lives, we reflect upon them in a purposeful way. We are always reflecting.

If you responded with a *yes* to the question of getting something out of what you reflect upon (or even if you are not sure), you are about to embark on a journey that will greatly change what you do with these reflections. In this book, I will guide you through a straightforward, but simple way to improve your life. How? By simply going beyond mere reflecting to taking committed actions regarding your reflective experiences. And what will be the results of these actions? Two things. One is growth, and second, a continuous forward movement toward your personal potential. Sound exciting? Why not get started today!

Made in the USA
Monee, IL
10 February 2022